Choose Your Life!

What readers are saying about Choose Your Life!

"I wanted to drop you a quick line of thanks and encouragement, for your book, *Choose Your Life!* that I enjoyed and valued so much. As a student of life, and practitioner of business, I have plenty of separate items to read about both topics. Your book is one of the few commentaries that puts them together and affords an insightful view about how one can truly share both a fulfilling career while living a value-rich and grounded life. Thanks for being a righteous and helpful messenger and please continue to provide your clarion calls for those of us toiling in the vineyards."

Partner of a large law firm in Atlanta, Georgia

***

"I wanted to drop you an email to let you know how much I have thoroughly enjoyed reading, absorbing, and applying *Choose Your Life!*. You have an uncanny way of taking dry principles and transforming them into specific actions that I then apply to both my personal and business life. In the very beginning of each chapter you ask deep and intriguing questions that stir my imagination. From the question of the number of tomorrows I have to knowing the difference between a fantasy and a vision, your questions enable me to dig deep and consider possibilities I have never thought of."

COO in Dallas, Texas

***

"I was impressed, touched, and encouraged by *Choose Your Life!* I have been so involved with what seems like a million things over the past few months that my life has been put on the backburner and this book is a reminder that there is hope and it is up to me to do something about it. Thanks again for a well written, clear, eye opening message."

Mother and homemaker in San Diego, California

***

"I thank you for your book because it does two great and unique things. First, it puts into plain language some practical, utilitarian ways in which honesty can pay off in the long run, which is something we rarely hear about. Second, it points out the remorse, even pain, one can feel for compromising one's principles. It's a convincing combination, one that may inspire someone, somewhere, to choose truth over lies, maybe even just once…and that, as you know yourself, is a powerful and positive thing"

CFO in Miami Florida

***

"My father just forwarded me your book as I sit here in my new "high-powered" office off of Fifth Avenue. Two weeks ago I received a promotion, and along with this massive complement came a stressful priority struggle. I have been in the office at 7:30 AM and leaving at 10:30 PM; I have been snapping at my friends and family each time they call to say something I have been thinking of as "a waste of time". I have not been able to do my laundry, let alone even drop it off at the Laundromat. My kitchen is a mess and I have lost 5 pounds due to lack of eating. This all leads up to the point: Your lovely book couldn't have arrived at a better time! Thank goodness I "made" the time to read it. I realize that if I don't sit down and write out my goals and priorities, not only will I have a nervous breakdown, but life will pass me by. At my funeral, it would be more important to hear that she 'always made times for her friends and family' than 'wow what a great project director'. Anyway, I just wanted to say thank you! "

Project Director, New York, New York

***

"All facets of my life have derived benefit from reading your book. In all of my life experiences, as an individual contributor to the director of a large call center for a Fortune 200 company, to my volunteerism with local charities, and to my most important roles of father and husband your book provides something meaningful. Thank you, Jim, for taking time to share yourself with me, and please accept my thanks for your commitment to developing the character and integrity of your community.

Senior Vice President in Dallas, Texas"

***

I never knew that I would learn so much about myself and how to live my life to the fullest by reading a book! Each time, I am excited to open it up because I get so much out of each chapter. You have a very comfortable style that allows me to truly get what you are saying. I feel like you are my personal coach allowing me to discover new things about myself through the simple yet meaningful points you make. The key to making your ideas work in my life is me listening to your call to action and then taking action. In your book, *Choose Your Life!,* I feel that you provide me with the encouragement and support I need to take my life to the next level. The fantastic thing is that each chapter focuses on one specific thing so that over time as I apply these principles I make progress toward becoming my dreams! Thank you for coaching me through your words!"

Managing Director in Dallas, Texas

***

"I just wanted to encourage you for your book, *Choose Your Life!* With the fall off in attendance by many in church or organized religious activities, your book may be one of the few ways in which business people are encouraged to be authentic, to live in the 'now' in the light of 'tomorrow' (not vice versa) and to get 'still' enough from time to time to examine their state of 'being' versus 'doing'. My observation is that many promising careers, marriages and other essential relationships (like being a dad) can be derailed when you continue to live life from the "outside-in" rather than from the "inside-out." Your book challenges business executives to be and permit others to be the 'whole person', and that encouragement is so needed today. Keep up the message—in fact, preach it brother, preach it!"

Partner in a large law firm in Atlanta, Georgia

***

"Your assistant shared your book, *Choose Your Life!* and I have now read all of it. I must say that understanding "life" as it pertains to business is usually the missing link in many people's lives. So many books are written on how to succeed in business but mention very little about how to incorporate life's lessons that combine all aspects into a truly gratifying accomplishment. Balance in life is vital and stumbling in different areas is a clear indication that one needs to be grounded in the simple lessons of life you teach in each chapter. I wish this was a mandatory read for everyone who thinks they can be successful without being grounded in reality. Thank you"

President in Chicago, Illinois

***

"A colleague of ours was kind enough to share with me your book, *Choose Your Life!*. I became a fan of yours after meeting you several times and attending one of your speaking engagements. I was very pleased to have found a resource that I can access that provides me the insight into how to be a successful business person. More importantly, your book helps me define and reinforce what it means to be successful as a person. Because you help define core values to make a life, not just a living, I am frequently referring others to your book as well."

Senior Vice President in Dallas, Texas

***

"*Choose Your Life!* is fantastic! The principles you have shared serve as a "touchstone," reminding leaders that we cannot lead our organizations beyond where we currently are without the courage to look inward. Each time I read them, I take pause and reflect on the decisions I make each day—as a leader, a father, and a friend."

COO in Dallas, Texas

JIM HULING

CHOOSE YOUR LIFE!

A POWERFUL, PROVEN METHOD FOR CREATING THE LIFE YOU WANT

2007

Choose Your Life!

TABLE OF CONTENTS

Acknowledgements	xvii
Introduction	xxiiii
Part I—The Questions that Matter	1
The Beginning	3
An Unexpected Defining Moment	4
A Moment of True Clarity	6
Who Are You?	9
Begin to Define the Life You Want	10
A Candid Assessment of Your Life Right Now	11
What Do You Really Want?	15
Deepen Your Vision	23
What Are You Prepared to Do?	31
Set a Major Goal for the Year	35
Decide How You Will Keep Score	36
Hold Yourself Accountable	37
Plan to Stay Engaged	37
Part II—Tools for the Journey	41
Wake Up Your Dreams	45
Remember the Dream	46
Brainstorm Ideas for Action	47
Imagine How You Would Feel if You Began to Pursue Your Dream	48
Harness the Power of Momentum to Make Your Dream Come True	48
Have the Courage to be Yourself	51
Are You Honest in Everything You Say?	52
Are You Honest When You Are Silent?	52
Are You Honest in the Image You Project?	53
Make Your Fear an Ally	55
State the Situation	56
Bring out Your Fears	56
Envision the Outcome You Want Most	59

Make a Choice   60
Overcome Your Fear of Change   61
You Will Decide What You Are Going to Focus on   61
You Will Decide What You Are Prepared to Do   62
You Will Decide Who You Will Become   62
Listen to Your Own Voice   65
Finding Your Way Home   66
Listen to Your Inner Voice   66
Take a Courageous First Step   69
Focus on The End   70
Have Faith   70
Take The First Step   70
Control Your Inner Dialog   73
Begin With Gratitude   74
Use Your Thoughts to Transform Your Relationships   74
Act With Conscious Kindness   77
The Power of Kindness Ripples Outward   78
Your Choices Define Who You Are   79
Know Whom to Trust   81
Find Strength in Your Vulnerability   83
Part III—Choosing Your Life Every Day   85
Create Treasured Memories   87
You Must Make Time for the Moments that Matter   88
Change Your Perspective   89
Begin to Create the Moments You Will Treasure   90
Character Versus Image   93
The High Price of Perfection   95
Set a Realistic Standard   96
Learn to Keep Score   96
Plan To Stay Engaged   96
The Cure for Exhaustion   97
Find a Deeper Connection to the People around You.   98
Find a Deeper Connection To Your Personal Excellence.   98
Find a Deeper Connection to Your Real Purpose.   98
Has Your Job Become Bigger Than Your Life?   99
Are Your responsibilities Overwhelming You?   99
Are You Secretly Afraid You're Not Qualified?   100

Is There No Room in Your Schedule for Your Life?   *100*

Are You Creating Your Own Crisis?   *101*

    Are You Creating Your Own Crisis?   *102*

    Are You Always Distracted?   *102*

Embracing Interruptions   *103*

    Life Doesn't Conform to Your Schedule.   *104*

    People Come to You Because They Believe You Can

      Help and that You Care.   *104*

    Staying Accessible and Available Keeps You Engaged.   *104*

Choose Carefully What You Carry   *105*

Invest Your Energy in What Matters Most   *107*

Reach Your Intended Destination   *111*

    Do You Know Your Exact Destination?   *111*

    Are You Following Your Guidance System?   *112*

Part IV—My Wish for You   113

Appendix 1—Forms   117

Who Are You?   *118*

What I Really Want   *119*

What I Am Prepared to Do   *120*

Dreams I Want to Awaken   *121*

Make Fear Your Ally   *122*

ACKNOWLEDGEMENTS

There are a few special people I want to thank in the creation of this book, to whom my gratitude is so deep that it almost overwhelms me. This book, like my life, is the culmination of your love and spirit. Thank you.

I want to first thank Dr. Stephen Covey, whose work has had a deep and profound impact on my life and on my leadership. Surely, I would not be where I am today, nor would I be the husband, father, and leader I am today, without your teaching. I also want to thank my dear friend, Bill Hickman ("the Captain"), for his friendship, his unceasing life force, his excellent coaching and counsel, and especially for his unique ability to rescue me when I need it most. Likewise, my thanks go to my friend Bill Hetherington, who continues to inspire me each day, and without whom my best ideas would never have come forth, in my writing, or in my leadership. Special thanks to Mick and Tricia Danskin at Danskin Creative Communication, not only for sharing their wonderful creative gifts in the cover design and forms, but also for their friendship and their passionate belief in the importance of this book. Thanks also to Bob Korch and Rick Sanders who patiently read each chapter on their own time and challenged me to make them better. To Bill Marianes, thank you for pushing me to pursue my gifts and for your constant friendship. To Dr. Betty Siegel, thank you for the inspiration of your life and for teaching me to simply love the audience before me. To Bill Gower, John Scarbrough, Ron McGinty, Lambert Chandler, and Frank Glenn, thank you for being great teachers, and for the privilege of being your CEO and your friend. To Jon Davis, thank you for walking across fire with me and for sharing the dream that became this book. To Dr. Richard Swindle, thank you for being one of the finest men I've ever known. Your friendship is very dear to me and your example can be found throughout the lessons in this book. To Philip Botha, who has taught me so much more than the art of fighting, thank you for the gift of your indomitable spirit—*Want some of this?*

Finally, and most importantly, thank you to my family. Almost thirty years ago, I married the most phenomenal woman I have ever known and to this day, I know it is the best choice I ever made. Donna, no aspect of my life is without the guiding influence of your wisdom and your care. Thank you, always, for the life-altering gift of your love. Sarah, you are a bright, shining, spectacular light in the world. Thank you for the privilege of standing in that light, sharing your journey, and being your dad. I love you with all my heart, sweet girl. Scott, you are a strong rock of a man whom I deeply respect and whose presence in my life I treasure. Thank you for being the man that you are and for never forgetting that life should be fun. I love you, son. And finally, thank you to my daughter-in-law Jennifer, and to my very special grandchildren Katie, Ian, and Maddie who have enabled me to begin a joyous new dimension of my life as Papa. I love you all.

To Donna, The True Love Of My Life
And To Sarah And Scott Who Made The Joy Deeper
I Love You All

INTRODUCTION

If I asked you to tell me about your life, what would you say? Would you begin with your name, your family status, or your job? *Hi, I'm Susan. I'm married to Dave and I'm a team leader at my company.* It's a comfortable answer and you usually offer it freely at everything from business meetings to neighborhood parties.

But what if I asked you to tell me about the *quality* of your life?

Most likely, you would offer a more revealing answer, and one that is not always so easy to give. *Well, I'd say it was pretty good. I mean, we all have our struggles, don't we? But all in all, I'd say things are going pretty well, most of the time. There are some things I'm working on, things that I need to do, but everybody has those. And there's some stuff I can't do anything about. I hope I can make some changes in the future, but I'd say good, overall.*

Not very inspiring, is it?

Now imagine for a moment how you would feel if you could answer the same question saying, *I'm living an extraordinary life.* Try it right now. Wherever you are, just say out loud, *I'm living an extraordinary life.* Now, say it again with real energy. ***I'm living an extraordinary life!***

Did you feel something when you said those words? Even if it was a little awkward, I believe you still felt something stir inside you, something that may have been asleep for a while.

At your core, what you want most is to live an extraordinary life. And by this, I mean a life that is extraordinary by your definition. I'm not referring to any preset standard of professional success, income, or lifestyle. **An extraordinary life is one that is lived true to the vision of your heart, whatever that may be.**

When you live in this way, you make an impact on the world. You know in the deepest part of your soul that you did all that was possible with the gifts you were given, that you had the courage to live your life as a great adventure, and most importantly, that your life mattered. And that's what you, and those around you, really want.

So, if this is what you want, are you doing it?

When you woke up this morning, were you excited to begin another day in your incredible life? Were you genuinely happy for just one more experience in your great adventure? If not, why not?

It could be almost anything—you're not feeling well, or you're worried about the pressures of your job, your kids aren't listening to you, the dishwasher needs repairing, you've got to walk the dog even though it's raining, and you just heard that traffic on your route into work is backed up for miles.

Everyone's life includes these things, and many more.

But here's the key: people who are living extraordinary lives experience these things as only a small part of a life filled with vision, with purpose, and with real excitement. It's not that they don't encounter difficulties and frustration; it's that they experience them in the context of a life so focused, so filled with purpose, that they cannot become real obstacles.

When you know who you are and what's important to you—when you know what you really want from all the dimensions of your life, and when you are actually making your dreams become reality in even the smallest ways each day—then the challenges you face become like footnotes in a compelling story. You see them, but your attention stays focused on the main story, on what's going to happen next.

So, how do you do it? How do you create a life that's extraordinary? You begin by knowing the answers to the questions that really matter.

Who are you?
What do you really want?
What are you prepared to do?

In Part I you'll take each of these questions and explore them deeply, giving you not only the understanding you need, but also practical exercises that will enable you to create your own compelling answers. You'll learn to define your life in terms of *LifeDimensions* and for each dimension you'll then build a *LifeVision*. At the end of Part I, you'll have a *LifePlan* unlike any you've ever encountered, one that is rooted in the deepest desires of your heart and one that will become a compelling force, taking you to the life you've always wanted.

Then, in Part II, you'll focus on the tools you will need along the way—essential skills such as how to turn fear into an ally, knowing whom to trust, and listening to your inner voice—tools that will enable you to succeed at creating your extraordinary life.

Finally, in Part III, you will experience a series of practical stories that illustrate how to apply these tools in living the life you've imagined—stories that will both inspire and challenge you to stay true to your vision by making the day-to-day choices that turn that vision into reality.

You know that a homing pigeon can be placed in a container with no ability to see, taken hundreds of miles away to an unknown destination, and when released, fly directly home. What you may not know yet is that, like the instincts of the homing pigeon, *there is a vision inside you of the life you want.*

Choose Your Life! will give you everything you need to awaken that vision and instill in you the same compelling drive to fly home to the life you were born to live.

Get ready to embark on the most exciting adventure of all—creating your extraordinary life.

PART I
The Questions that Matter

Who are you?

Who are you, really? Beyond all surface labels, who is the unique soul that is really you? What's important to you? What are the core values that define you? What is the relative priority of the different dimensions of your life and which ones are truly most important?

What do you really want?

What do you really want from your life? Can you describe what you want in vivid, precise detail? Do you have a vision so exciting that you are compelled to live it out?

What are you prepared to do?

Are you prepared to go beyond thinking, and dreaming, and talking about the life you want to actually living it? Are you willing to be accountable for staying true to your vision?

THE BEGINNING

The story of my own extraordinary life

In the early '80s, I was a member of a cult. It was a worldwide movement with membership in the hundreds of thousands requiring total devotion to its cause. Although you might have known of it as one of the eight largest accounting firms in the world, believe me, for those of us who worked there it was a cult.

I had recently completed my education and like so many other young people, I was full of ambition and a burning desire to create a great career and a great life. My only problem was that I had absolutely no idea how to do it. It was frightening to be out in the real world and away from the womb of college—with the sobering realization that now it was all up to me. I would either make it, or I wouldn't. And believe me, I really wanted to make it.

The cult leaders were experts at drawing in young people exactly like me. They certainly appeared to know the secret to creating a great life. After all, they had everything that usually defines success—money, recognition, power—and they were willing to share it. All I had to do was join and they would teach me everything I needed to know to have the life I wanted. *Sign here, son. Welcome to the firm.*

I couldn't sign fast enough. If they had asked for a drop of blood, I would have opened a vein.

It wasn't long before I realized that in every assignment, every memo, and every performance review, their "secret" for creating a great life came down to a single overriding message: *Your job is the most important thing in your life.* As a young, ambitious professional, it was easy to believe the message, and once I started to believe it, I was hooked. I worked seventy, eighty, and sometimes one hundred hours per week, traveled from Sunday to Friday, and said yes to every new opportunity. All because I really believed that my job was the most important thing in my life. Of course, if you had asked me what was important in my life, I would have told a different story. But my actions revealed my true answer.

An Unexpected Defining Momnt

After several years of this life, I was sitting alone one night in my hotel reading a new book titled *The 7 Habits of Highly Successful People.* In one of the early chapters, the author, Dr. Stephen Covey, suggested something radical: that we define our lives not by our jobs, but by the things we care most about. A message very different from the one I was living.

Following the direction of the book, I sat at the small desk in my hotel room and made a list of all the things that were important to me in terms of the dimensions of my life: Donna's Husband, Scott and Sarah's Dad, Business Leader, Martial Artist, Writer, Friend and many others.

As I looked at the list I had created, I experienced one of the true defining moments of my life. I was struck by how many aspects of my life were important to me beyond my job. My work was, and still is important to me, but the revelation I had that night was realizing how deeply I cared about all the other roles on that list, and more importantly, how little I was investing in them. It was literally a defining moment in my life for which I will always be grateful to Dr. Covey, because it changed me forever.

Sitting in that hotel room, looking at that list, I resolved that somehow, I would find a way to invest in all of these roles, to become the father, husband, and friend I knew I wanted to be, while still pursuing a career that mattered to me.

To start, I needed a vision of everything I wanted for these roles in my life. To get this vision, clearly and completely, I again followed the advice of Dr. Covey to *begin at the end*—to literally imagine the words I would want said as my eulogy, spoken by the person who was the primary focus of the role.

I decided to start with the role of father to my beautiful baby girl, Sarah, and my handsome young son, Scott. Sitting alone at the hotel desk, I closed my eyes and let my imagination take over. In my mind, I saw Sarah and Scott, many years in the future, standing in front of our friends and family at my funeral service. They were about to describe what their relationship with their dad had meant to them. It was a sobering image, imagining my infant daughter and my young son fully grown, with all the years between now and then over and finished. With my imagination running like a film in my mind, I saw them look directly at those who had gathered, tears filling their eyes.

On the tablet in front of me, I wrote the first thing Sarah and Scott would say in that moment. It was one sentence, but it was a sentence that changed my life. I imagined each of them saying, *My dad was always there for me.*

Only, I wasn't there. I was sitting in a distant city, away from them as I had often been, giving everything to my job.

As I stared at that sentence my heart broke open. Everything that I knew I wanted to be to Scott and Sarah came pouring out in pages and pages of the most visionary experience I have ever had. With tears staining each page, I wrote about the kind of dad I wanted to be. I wrote about the adventures I wanted to share with them, how much I wanted them to trust me and know that they could always depend on me, and all that we would mean to each other throughout our lives...because their dad had always been there.

Days later, I walked into cult headquarters and resigned from a job that required hundred-hour weeks and constant travel. From that day forward, I knew my job would never again be the most important thing in my life.

Looking back on this moment in my career, I realize that I might handle it differently today; the word *transition* comes to mind, doesn't it? But what I want you to understand is that on that day, with the pages of my eulogy in my jacket pocket, I had a vision so clear, so real, so compelling, that I had no choice but to live it out. I could not, and I would not, wait another day to begin.

Can you imagine this feeling? When you woke this morning, were you compelled by a vision for your life, one that made you excited to begin another day? Was your heart filled with gratitude for just one more chance to live out the vision you've created? Or did you wake up hoping to just get through another day?

When you have a vision for your life—when you really know what you want, and are making the choices that bring that vision into reality—it's like a guiding hand that literally pulls you through your life. Most people live each day through effort, obligation, and sheer will to do what they have to do. But people who have a vision for their lives are always creating something they know they want, and each step in that journey is a joyous adventure.

I'm not saying that it isn't a lot of work. It is. But it's work with a purpose, work with meaning, work that constantly reminds you that you're living the life you've dreamed of. And it's the most joyous experience you can imagine.

In all the years that have now passed, Sarah, Scott, and I have lived out everything that I envisioned in that hotel room long ago, from dozens of backpacking trips and rock-climbing expeditions, to kayaking and white-water rafting trips, earning our black belts in Taekwondo, and on, and on. And through all that we have shared, we built the deep love and connection that was so important to me that it changed the direction of my life.

Today, I could tell the same story of a vision lived out as husband of almost thirty years to the most phenomenal woman I have ever known, my wife, Donna. I could tell about living my vision as CEO of a highly successful company, of becoming an advanced martial artist, a keynote speaker, a published author, and many others.

In each of these roles, I have done the inner work to have a clear vision of what I want and each day I navigate my life toward the fulfillment of all I've dreamed of becoming.

This book not only contains a record of my journey, it also contains the personal method I've developed through nearly thirty years of intentional living. Beginning with the insight I gained alone in that hotel room, I have sought out and applied many ideas and techniques, using them as springboards to ultimately create my own unique method of living. *Choose Your Life!* **embodies the best of all I have learned and a true roadmap of what has worked for me.**

A Moment of True Clarity

It wasn't long ago that another defining moment confirmed the value of a life lived with purpose and vision. On a Sunday evening, I was sitting in one of my favorite restaurants with Donna and Sarah, enjoying an excellent meal. Virtually every aspect of my life was going beautifully, from my family, to my career and my health. Truly, I was riding the crest of the wave.

Three hours later, I was lying in an ambulance with no heartbeat registering on the monitor. A severe food reaction had spiked my fever and literally made my heart stop. When I regained consciousness, I looked out the glass panels of the ambulance door to see Donna and Sarah following closely behind as we sped to the nearest hospital. With all my soul, I believed that this was to be my last moment on earth. And in that moment, as I saw their faces and held in my heart the face of my son, Scott, I had a startling revelation...*I had no regrets.*

Can you imagine this feeling? Lying in an ambulance, absolutely certain that these are your last moments on earth, and feeling an overwhelming sense of peace and gratitude?

Truly, it was a miracle.

Don't misunderstand me. Without question, I wanted more days to live, and I knew that there were things I would do differently and better, given the chance.

But what I'm saying is that *I had lived the life I wanted to live*. I had loved the people in my life with all my heart. I had spent time with them and had truly been present. I had also pursued my life's work with passion and dedication, found activities that I loved and made time for them, and had given myself to those causes that were important to me.

If this moment was to be my last, then I would pass from this world to the next knowing that I had done what I wanted to do. No regrets.

Isn't this what you want? Isn't this what everyone wants?

I believe it is. I know you will believe it too if you only imagine the countless thousands who, in that moment, would wish for one more day, one more chance to go back and be the people they wanted to be, to say the things they always wanted to say—literally, to live the lives they wanted to live.

I've found a way to create this kind of extraordinary life and I probably have no greater talent, drive, or ability than you do right now. The only difference between us is that I have a plan and a way to pursue it every day. And that's why I have written this book: to share with you what I've learned.

I want you to have your own extraordinary life, one that will enable your last moment, when it comes, to be one of joy with no regrets. But I also want you to make each moment from this day to that the most fulfilling and exciting experience you can imagine.

Everything contained in this book comes down to three questions. I call them **The Questions That Matter**. And I believe that they are the most important you can ever answer:

Who are you?
What do you really want?
What are you prepared to do?

The chapters that follow will introduce you to these questions in a powerful way. But here's a warning: you can't just read them and think that you've got it. Finding your own answers will take work. So, I've included exercises in each chapter to enable you to go deeper, to challenge yourself, and begin the process of really answering these questions, perhaps for the first time in your life.

As I look back across the decades of my life, I see the results of having a clear vision and intentionally pursuing it every day, and I know with absolute certainty that it has been worth it.

I have seen many other approaches to life, and I have had the gift of seeing the results of those approaches over time. I've known many individuals, for example, who dedicated themselves exclusively to their careers, channeling all of their time and energy toward this one objective. Many of them have become high-ranking executives and have achieved great things professionally. However, they paid a high price in terms of meaningful relationships, personal health, and inner peace that, for me would not have been success, regardless of my title or income. And because you're reading this book, I don't believe it would be for you either.

For us, success is a life that is filled with work we are passionate about, but also with meaningful relationships, with dreams that come true, and ultimately, with the clear conviction that we are living the life we were meant to live.

It's an amazing journey. Let's get started.

WHO ARE YOU?

Set the direction of your life by creating a deeper definition of who
you are

I don't have time to plan my life. I'm too busy deciding where to eat. Sound ridiculous? Think for a moment of all the cumulative hours that you've spent choosing a restaurant: *What do you want? I don't know. What do you want? Fast food? Take out? Italian? Chinese?*

You know the dialog by heart. Now, contrast that with the total time you've invested in mapping the course of your life—not daydreaming— but actually creating a vision of who you want to become, what you want to do, and what it all means. Where have you spent more time?

I know the answer because I was there once. I also know what happened in my life when I became clear about what I wanted: a miracle.

The first step in creating an extraordinary life is about setting a clear direction for your life before spending years running the race. And you're going to do it by answering a question that is deceptively simple: *Who are you?*

Have you ever had the experience of knowing people casually for a while, perhaps at work, and then finding out that they were passionately interested in something that was also an interest of yours? Before that moment, you probably knew only the surface-level characteristics that identified them: married, project manager, two kids, etc. But once you learned that they shared this passion, your relationship began to deepen; you felt you really knew them for the first time. Throughout the remainder of this book, we'll refer to these deeper definitions as *LifeDimensions.*

This process of discovery is the same process you will use to set the direction of your life. But in this case, the person you will be discovering more about is you. What are you passionate about? Whom do you love? What's most important to you? The first step in creating an extraordinary life is discovering the answers to questions like these, and in the process, creating a deeper definition of who you really are.

Try it right now. There's a special form in the Appendix at the end of this book titled *Who Am I?* that will help you work through the exercises in this chapter as well as a version you can download at www.JimHuling.com/forms. Get a copy of it in front of you before you read any further.

Begin to Define the Life You Want

Use the form to list the *LifeDimensions* you care most about. Remember to include everything, from family, to work, to personal activities as well as your involvement in causes that matter to you. Don't try to be too precise at this point; we'll refine the list later. Just be sure the list includes all the things that matter to you.

Your list may include *LifeDimensions* that relate to your family such as dad, mom, sister, son, fiancée, or aunt. It may also include dimensions that express your daily work such as manager, homemaker, graphic artist, accountant, or vice president. Once you've written these, think about other dimensions like softball coach, spiritual seeker, room mother, athlete, or friend. For example, my list includes *LifeDimensions* such as Donna's Husband, Sarah and Scott's Dad, CEO, Martial Artist, and Friend, among others.

Now take a moment to make each *LifeDimension* more meaningful by personalizing it. For me, there is a real difference in the dimension of *husband,* as opposed to *Donna's husband.* I'm not just anybody's dad; I'm Scott's dad and Sarah's dad. Including this extra personalization will bring in a level of emotion that makes it more powerful in defining your life. Make sure you add this personalization to each *LifeDimension* where it applies.

Finally, review the list to ensure it has every *LifeDimension* you want your identity to include, even if you're not investing in it right now. For example, if you know that the true definition of who you are includes being a writer, then make sure it's on your list, even if you're not writing anything yet.

Now, take a look at the life you've started to define.

You're probably struck first by how many *LifeDimensions* you listed beyond the basics. Do you feel a sense of excitement when you think of your life including these various dimensions? Sometimes just seeing them written down is a breakthrough moment; a feeling inside of you that says *Yes! That's the life I want!*

This moment is almost always followed by a more sobering one when you think, *But how will I ever do it all?* Don't worry about that yet. Remember, in this exercise you're setting the direction for your life. Later, you'll make a plan for the journey and I'll show you how to integrate regular engagement in all your *LifeDimensions* into your daily routine.

Before you continue, look once more across the list of your *LifeDimensions*. Did you list a dimension that you once dreamed of but had forgotten? This happens often. When you finally slow down to ask yourself real questions, you start to get real answers. And you remember the dreams you once had before the pressures of your day-to-day responsibilities started to consume you. Reawakening these forgotten dreams is a vital component of creating your extraordinary life and one that you'll spend focused time on later.

For now, you need to keep working on the definition of who you are.

A Candid Assessment of Your Life Right Now

Now it's time for some sobering work. Take another look at your list and think back over how you've spent your time in the past month. Place a check mark beside each *LifeDimension* where you invested five or more hours in the last thirty days.

How many *LifeDimensions* had no check mark? Stunning, isn't it? An exercise like this clearly reveals the gap between the life you want to live and the life you are really living. You've probably invested more time in your favorite television series than in some of these *LifeDimensions* that define the real you.

To go a step further, circle the *most important LifeDimension* that does NOT have a check mark beside it. This is what's called a BFO—a Blinding Flash of the Obvious. Usually, the particular *LifeDimension* that is circled is a source of real pain, both because it's truly important to you, and because the inescapable reality is that you are doing almost nothing about it. Accumulate enough of these and your deathbed experience will be one giant BFO of all you missed in life.

If you want to change this picture, then you're ready to make a new list.

Take all the *LifeDimensions* you've identified and assign them an absolute priority using the column on your form. Start with the

JIM HULING

dimension that is the single most important one in your life and put the number 1 beside it, then continue to number the *LifeDimensions* in order of decreasing importance. Let me warn you, this is difficult work if you're serious about it. Placing one dimension above another in importance can be heartrending, but it is work you need to do.

Deciding what's really important is the single most powerful way to answer the question *Who are you?* Like a compass pointing north, knowing who you really are sets the direction for life. But if you live with the fantasy that *everything is number 1,* then nothing really is. Assigning a relative priority forces you to decide how important each dimension truly is. It also enables you to begin to know yourself more completely and to make real decisions about where you will invest your time and energy.

With your priorities assigned, you're ready for the final step: evaluating where you are in each *LifeDimension.* Use the final column on your form to assign a letter grade of A for excellent, B for good, C for mediocre, D for poor, and F for failing.

You'll notice that I've redefined C from the traditional label of "average" to "mediocre." For me, there is false comfort in calling yourself average. It implies you're living at a standard which, although not great, is acceptable. This comfort zone is like quicksand—it can pull you down before you know it to a life that brings no joy or fulfillment. In the end, average is really another label for *failing with companionship.* While you might have been temporarily satisfied with being average, you won't be when you label it mediocre.

Remember also that these grades are your own. Don't try to think about the grade that anyone else would give you. They may be judging based on the image you maintain and not on the real quality of your life. Hold yourself more brutally accountable by measuring yourself against your own inner standard.

So, how does your report card look? If you're like most people you have some dimensions where you're performing well and others where more investment is needed. Don't worry. In the chapters that follow, you'll develop a clear vision for each *LifeDimension* and then a plan for making that vision a reality.

For now, finish this exercise by drawing a circle around those *LifeDimensions* that have both the <u>highest</u> importance ranking (remember that 1 is the *highest* importance ranking) and the <u>lowest</u> grade. These circles will highlight the areas of your life that are probably causing you the most pain and dissatisfaction. They are also the areas where an improvement will mean the most to you.

***

Congratulations! You've just spent more time thinking about your life than most people do in a decade. Your definition of who you are through these *LifeDimensions*, your understanding of which of them is most important, and your candid assessment of how you're doing in each of them is a very strong beginning.

From this beginning, you are already better prepared to choose how you will live. The title of this book—*Choose Your Life!*—has two important meanings related to this.

First, you must *choose your life* in the sense that it's *your* life, not someone else's, that you're living Until you understand yourself and what's important to you more deeply, you are more likely to adopt the definition and the priorities offered by your parents, your spouse, or your company. Whether good or bad, this definition will never be *your life*, and as a result, will never bring you fulfillment.

Second, you must literally *choose* the life you want, in hundreds of individual moments throughout every day. You must be willing to make the choice, but you also need a guide to ensure that the choices you make will result in the life you want. Defining who you really are is the beginning.

You can live your life *on purpose* with a sense of identity and direction, or you can just show up every day and try to hit life's curveballs. The more deeply you do the work outlined in this chapter, the more deeply you will know yourself, and this knowledge will be the foundation on which you can begin to build your extraordinary life.

Recognizing and accepting who you are may not be easy, but it is the essential first step in choosing your life. Before you turn the page, pause for a moment to contemplate what you have done. Answering the question *Who are you?* required you to look deeply inside yourself. The next step in choosing your life will require you to use that skill to look forward, with purpose and faith, to answer the question *What do you really want?*

WHAT DO YOU REALLY WANT?

Take control of your life by building a compelling vision

How many tomorrows do you have? Thousands? One? The answer is that you don't know. But the real question is about how you are living your life. Are you assuming there will always be a tomorrow to do what you want to do, to become the person that you want to be?

As I shared in the opening chapter, one fateful night I was having dinner with my wife and daughter at a favorite restaurant and life couldn't have been more perfect. And then, a few hours later, severe food poisoning sent me to an emergency room with my blood pressure crashing and my family watching a monitor that failed to register a heartbeat. Did I wish for the chance to send one more e-mail, review one more report, or attend one final meeting? *Of course not*, you're probably thinking.

But what about you? Isn't that what you do day after day as you're working late, taking cell phone calls at dinner, and canceling your vacation? And on a deeper level, are you holding back on giving yourself to the people you love, developing your gifts and talents, and investing in causes that matter to you, waiting for a more convenient time to begin?

If you are, then you are making these decisions on the assumption that there will always be a tomorrow to create the life you want. And then one day when you least expect it, your tomorrows are gone.

Do you know what you *really* want?

Here's a powerful exercise to enable you to answer this question:

I have been given the miraculous ability to fulfill your three greatest desires for your life. The only catch is that you must state them in the next sixty seconds exactly as you want them fulfilled. Only three desires can be fulfilled and you can't ask for more. Go!

Did you know what to ask for? Your first reaction was probably to ask for more time. After all, you're given only three desires to have fulfilled, so that makes each one really important. You've only got sixty seconds, so you have to think about a lot of things: the people you care about, what you want to do with your life, what you need to be happy. Then you have to be sure that you know which of these things is the most important since you can choose only three desires to have fulfilled. Finally, you need to be able to say them with real clarity because they will be fulfilled exactly as you state them and you don't want to leave anything out.

It's a tough exercise, isn't it? Welcome to life.

The exercise I've just described is the process by which you live. Each day you make the choices that define who you are and what you really want. With every choice you set your trajectory toward a specific outcome. The only question is will you make those choices unconsciously, hoping that everything turns out okay in the end, or will you take responsibility from this moment forward for choosing exactly the life you want? In the end, your choices will tell the story of what was most important to you, regardless of your intentions.

Why not do the work to discover what you want most? You can start right now to take control of the direction of your life by building a compelling *LifeVision*.

Look back over the *LifeDimensions* you defined in the last chapter and choose one to work on. You may want to choose the dimension that you ranked as first in importance, or you may want to choose the one that you circled as having the greatest gap between importance and your current performance. Whichever one you choose, be sure it's one you're highly interested in developing, since it will be the focus of the exercises you will do from this point forward.

Now, think about what you really want in this *LifeDimension*. What kinds of experiences do you want to share? What do you want the relationship to have meant throughout your life? Who do you want to become in fulfilling this dimension of your life?

These questions are deep and at first, can be overwhelming. To really answer them, I encourage you to use the same approach I used that night in my hotel room: *begin at the end*. The single most powerful way to discover all you want in any dimension of your life is to develop a *LifeVision*. To do this, you must imagine what you want the people in your life to be able to say about who you were, how you lived, and what you meant to them when there are no more tomorrows left for you to get it right. But I want to warn you, this is not for the faint of heart.

First, find a quiet place to do this work and dedicate a block of time when you know you won't be interrupted.

There's a special form in the Appendix at the end of this book titled *What I Really Want* that will help you work through the exercises in this chapter as well as a version you can download at www.JimHuling.com/forms. Get a copy of it in front of you to help in capturing your vision.

This form is designed to get your thoughts flowing and to open your heart to all you can imagine your life including. It won't be the final version of your *LifeVision* for this dimension, but it will help you discover some of your deepest desires so that you can include them when you write your complete vision.

The first section focuses on what you want to *be*. When you work on this section, think of all the characteristics you want to embody in this dimension of your life and list them in the space provided. Later, you'll refine this list into a more complete set of characteristics, but for now, just let your thoughts flow. For example, in living the *LifeDimension* of Scott and Sarah's Dad, I want to be a dad who is:

Loving
Open-hearted
Always there
Dependable
Fun
Fully engaged

The next section focuses on what you to *do*. Completing this section can be a lot of fun as you let your imagination picture all the things you'd like to do in this dimension of your life. Staying with the *LifeDimension* of Scott and Sarah's Dad, some examples of the things I want to *do* are:

- *Have regular one-on-one time with no distractions*
- *Share great adventures like rafting the Salmon River or backpacking in Alaska*
- *Sit around a campfire on a starry night and tell stories*
- *Really talk about life without coming across as the parent*
- *Set a goal together (like earning our black belts or running a 10k) and achieve it*

- *Find a community service project that we're passionate about and get involved together*

The final section focuses on what you want to *learn*. Here's where you can envision the great lessons of your life and how you might apply them in this dimension. Think of the areas where knowledge, expertise, or wisdom will enable you to live the life you've imagined. In my *LifeDimension* of Scott and Sarah's Dad, here are some of the things I want to learn.

- *I want to learn how to really listen to my kids, without thinking about work or anything else in the background.*
- *I want to learn how to survive in the wilderness so that I can help if we're ever lost while backpacking.*
- *I want to learn how to share my failures as easily as my successes and to be open and vulnerable.*
- *I want to learn how to guide a raft so that we can go on great adventures together.*

When you've spent time thinking about these three areas, as well as beginning to imagine what you really want to be, do, and learn, you're ready to begin crafting your *LifeVision* for this dimension. You'll use all of the material on this form in the next stage, but now, you'll go deeper.

When you're ready, begin by picturing the face of the person who is the focus of this *LifeDimension* for you. This could be your husband or wife, your son or daughter, a close friend, or someone you've worked with, so long as he or she is the individual who most clearly defines the focus of this dimension for you.

Now see the person standing before your friends and family, one day far in the future. In your imagination, see the person walking to the front of the room and saying, *I'd like to tell all of you what my relationship with (fill in your name or the name by which they would refer to you, e.g., my dad/mom/husband/friend) meant to me.*

Then write the words that come from your heart. Don't hold back. Write everything that you will want this person to say—everything you care about, hope for, and dream will come true. Write about the relationship you had, the adventures you shared, the times when you laughed together, and the times when you revealed your deepest heartache. Give this person the words you will want him or her to be able to say about your life and how much it mattered. Get it all out on paper now. Write as though your life depended on it. It does.

As you do this exercise, use real language just as the person would say it today. Resist the temptation to settle for lofty words such as *she was a great person who dedicated herself to the highest use of her talents and to serving the common good.* Not only is this meaningless, it carries no *emotional content.* And without emotional content, you'll be missing the spark that will inspire you to want make this vision of your life a reality.

If you don't feel emotional content in the words you're writing, it's a good indication that you are writing from your head, not your heart. When you write using only your mind, you limit yourself to saying what's safe and predictable, what others would think was appropriate, instead of what you really want. If this is all you do, in the end you will have only words, words that carry no inspiration at all.

But if you can make the infinite twelve-inch journey from your mind down to your heart, you can tap into a deep well of emotion, of desire, and of passion. When *those* words start coming out, you'll know it, because you won't just be writing, you'll be feeling all you want to say. This may take several sessions to achieve, with each one taking you to a deeper level of truth and meaning. Be patient. I promise, it will be worth it.

When I wrote my *LifeVision* as Scott and Sarah's Dad, I started by imagining each of them saying, *My dad was always there for me.* It was a sentence that changed my life, because it tapped into my greatest desire, which was to truly be a great dad to Sarah and to Scott. *This* was what I really wanted with a passion so deep that when I started writing, I couldn't stop. I then went on to write about how much we loved each other, the times we shared, and all the things we would do together. I remember crying most of the way through it. And today, over twenty years later, the pages are still stained with tears.

Later I went on to write an equally important *LifeVision* that captured my true desire to be a great husband to my wife, Donna, an example I will reference later in this book.

In expressing my greatest desire through these *LifeVisions*, I also had to confront the source of my greatest pain. I really had to see that working and traveling almost 100 percent of my time was forcing me to put off until tomorrow becoming a great husband and dad. This conclusion may seem obvious, but many of the people I know are doing the same thing: responding to the urgent demands of their work at the expense of their lives.

Today, I have a written *LifeVision* of what I really want in every dimension of my life—as Donna's husband, CEO of my company, and many others. These vision statements are the defining charter of my life— a meaningful and passionate bedrock definition of each *LifeDimension* that defines me. They give my life focus and a sense of meaning, and they enable me to live with a sense of purpose, knowing that I'm creating the life I want.

Developing a vision for each dimension of your life is the most important work you will ever do. Is it a demanding assignment? Yes. I won't mislead you. But in the scope of your life you will spend less time creating your vision than you will watching your favorite series on television. It's not a question of the work involved. It's a question of how intentionally you want to live your life.

An unexpected trip to an emergency room reminded me that none of us is guaranteed a single tomorrow. Don't wait. Start today to create a vision of your extraordinary life.

***

If you want the writing of your *LifeVision* to be an experience that changes your life, remember these things:

1. *Start with a LifeDimension that matters most to you.* Eventually you will develop a vision for every dimension of your life, but starting with one that you are most passionate about will launch you strongly into this process.

2. *Choose a place to write where you can be alone and undisturbed.*

3. *Allocate a minimum of one hour.*

4. *Write the words as the person who is the focus of this dimension would say them.* For example, if it's your son, he would say *my dad*, instead of Jim. Write it as a script that he would read, not as a factual report.

5. *Use real language.* The loftier the language, the less meaningful the content.

6. *Be specific.* There's a real difference in your spouse saying, *He was a thoughtful person*, and saying, *Every Friday that I can remember he would walk through the door with flowers in his hand. Sometimes it was a big bouquet and sometimes it was just a bunch of wildflowers that he'd picked on the way home that still had ants crawling on them. But the important thing was that he remembered. It was his way of saying I love you.* I know you can feel the difference.

7. *Most important of all, find your own emotional content.* Without it, your words will have no real impact. If you don't feel anything when you read them, you're not there yet. But also remember that emotional content comes in layers. You may need several sessions to finally drill down to your real core of passion and desire. When you do, I promise it will be worth the effort.

DEEPEN YOUR VISION

Discover the characteristics of the person you want to become

Not long ago I had lunch with Susan, a successful managing partner at a large financial services firm. After she recounted closing a major deal with a new client, celebrating her tenth year of marriage, becoming president of her nonprofit association, and agreeing to serve as room mother for both her children's classes, she paused, and looked at me with tear-filled eyes.

"I'm exhausted," she said. "I feel like I'm running as fast as I can but I'm not really getting anywhere. I'm not even sure what it all means anymore."

Can you relate to her story? Are you living your life doing all the *right* things, filling your days with endless good works, excellence in your job, selfless dedication to your family and your causes, and a desperate need to say yes to every request? When was the last time you stopped your frenzied, over-achieving pace to ask yourself the most important question underlying everything you do: *Why?* Without this answer, even the noblest of activities can lose their meaning and leave you lost and exhausted.

On the other hand, if you know what you want from your life, if a clear and compelling vision guides you, you can gradually begin to increase the activities that fulfill that vision and decrease those that don't. The difference is not in which activities you do; the difference is in *why you do them*.

And this is why you must continue working hard on the vision you began to create in the last chapter.

If you haven't yet created a written *LifeVision* for at least one dimension of your life, I encourage you to stop reading now and go back to the last chapter. However, if you're struggling to allocate the time this takes, then look in the mirror and ask yourself some candid questions:

Are you living exactly the life you want to live? If not, then isn't it time to start defining who you are, what you really want, and what you are prepared to do to make it happen?

Do you have the courage to redefine your life? The hard truth is that many people don't. It's simply easier to abandon your life to the frenetic activity that is demanded by all the external forces that surround you. But don't confuse this with not having enough time. You have the time. What you may lack is the courage or the will. Only you can decide.

Here's the best advice I can give you: **Do the work.** Nothing in your life will change until you do. Real change, fulfillment, and joy are waiting for you on the other side of this process and all it takes to get there is time spent exploring what you really want.

If you've written a vision statement for one of your *LifeDimensions*, even if it's still a work in progress, then you're ready to move on to the next step.

Start by reading through the vision you've written and making a list of the individual characteristics that it contains. You started with some of these characteristics in the first exercise when you were imagining what you wanted to *be, do, and learn.* Now that you've expanded that into your *LifeVision,* you'll find these characteristics evident throughout the passionate words that you wrote, even though they are in narrative style. When you list the characteristics now, they will become a succinct reminder of all that you wrote, and of all that you want to be and do as you fulfill this vision for your life.

For example, do you remember the excerpt in the last chapter about bringing home flowers?

Every Friday that I can remember he would walk through the door with flowers in his hand. Sometimes it was a big bouquet and sometimes it was just a bunch of wildflowers that he'd picked on the way home that still had ants crawling on them. But the important thing was that he remembered. It was his way of saying I love you.

This is an actual segment of my *LifeVision* as Donna's Husband that I wrote to illustrate one aspect of the type of husband I wanted to be. But if I want to use this segment to create a plan for my life, I need to make it more precise by distilling it down to the specific characteristic it embodies. In the end, it's living the characteristic, rather than the literal example of flowers, that will make me the husband I want to be. Once I truly embody the characteristic, I may find dozens of ways to express it.

So, as an example, I can distill the segment about flowers down to the one-word characteristic of *thoughtful*. In this same way, I can distill other parts of my *LifeVision* as Donna's husband into characteristics such as *great listener, romantic,* and *fun.*

Be careful not to think of the list of characteristics as a substitute for the vision, because it's the vision that gives you a complete definition of all that you want. If you had created only a list of characteristics to work on, it would be just another list of things to do. Writing the narrative enabled you to speak from your heart and create a rich, vibrant picture of this area of your life that, hopefully, has the emotional content to inspire you to action.

While the *LifeVision* gives you the *why,* isolating the characteristics gives you the *what* in a simple and concise form. And it's powerful because it's *your* list, not one that anyone else imposed on you.

In the end, what makes this way of approaching life so different is that it begins with the heart. Every action, every plan, every strategy you will develop through this book will be rooted in your unique desires for your life, not in someone else's idea of what you *should* be or do. As a result, you'll have very few moments in your life when you do something solely out of obligation with no meaning or purpose.

To continue this example, here's a partial list of the characteristics I can draw out of my vision for being Donna's Husband:

Thoughtful
Great listener
Romantic
Fun

Becoming a husband (or a wife or partner) who fully embodies just these four characteristics might be one of the most significant things you could ever strive for in a relationship. Of course, your list might be different. But for a moment, imagine what it would be like to hear your spouse describing you in terms of these characteristics.

He was just so thoughtful. If I asked him to do something, he always did it, but it's wasn't just that. He saw the things I needed or wanted and did them without me ever mentioning it. When he would leave early for a business trip, he would put a card on the pillow next to me while I was sleeping that said how much he would miss me while he was away. When he came home, he would have a special gift.

How would it make you feel if someone could say this about you?

Whether or not this segment, which is taken from my *LifeVision* as Donna's Husband, matches the kind of spouse or partner you want to be, you can see what is most important to me: that she feels loved through these actions. But unless you are a very, very special person, these things don't happen spontaneously. You have to grow into these characteristics, and to do that, you need a plan. Once you've isolated your list of characteristics, you are ready to begin creating your *LifePlan.*

Start by taking one characteristic from your vision and brainstorming all the action ideas you can think of that would enable you to live it out. In other words, think of the things you could start doing right now that would close the gap between where you are today and where you want to be.

A list of ideas for the characteristic of *thoughtful* might look like this:

Thoughtful

- *Leave a card on the pillow for each business trip*
- *Whenever she asks me to do something, write it down so I don't forget, and then make sure I do it*
- *Watch for things that she needs or wants and keep a specific list in my day planner that includes brands, sizes, colors, etc.*
- *Always bring something home from a trip, even if it's a single flower*
- *Each week do something that is normally her responsibility without being asked and without making a big deal about it*

This is just an excerpt drawn from my own desire to be a husband who is thoughtful, but I've used it to illustrate the kinds if ideas you're searching for in this exercise. Your unique vision of who you want to be as a husband, wife, partner, or friend will be different. Put all your energy into forming your own list of ideas, things you can actually do to start becoming the person reflected in the words and feelings of your *LifeVision*.

Thus far, I've focused on an example that is personal, but remember that this process applies equally well if you've chosen to create a vision for your work. Here's a brief example of my vision for my dimension as CEO of my company. It describes some of what I hope to be and do by the time I retire from this position.

A few of the characteristics I want to embody as a leader are:

Leadership Characteristics

Authentic
Approachable
Courageous
Great Listener
Compassionate
Committed

If I take the characteristic of *authentic*, I can then brainstorm ideas that will enable me to become a leader who embodies authenticity, such as:

Authentic

- *Develop a clear set of written values and be sure others know about them.*
- *At the end of each day, evaluate my actions and my decisions against my values to be sure I am consistent*
- *Tell the truth, no matter how difficult*
- *Set up an anonymous feedback method so that the people I work with can hold me accountable*
- *Treat everyone with respect and appreciation, regardless of his or her position in the company*

Just as in the example of my dimension as Donna's Husband, these characteristics and ideas may or may not be the things you would want to do as a leader. It doesn't matter. What matters is that you develop your own vision for each dimension in your life and then make it real by identifying the characteristics you want your life to illustrate.

When you've finished brainstorming a list of ideas for each

characteristic, you're ready to move on to the next chapter. But before you do, let's sum up the process so far to be sure it's clear:

1. In Chapter 2, you identified the dimensions that make up your life, including those you are actively investing in now, and those you want to begin investing in, to create the life you want.

2. You then worked with that list of *LifeDimensions* to identify which are the most important to you and to understand how you are investing your time.

3. Out of the list of *LifeDimensions*, you chose the one you wanted to work on first, one that was particularly important to you.

4. In Chapter 3, you developed a *LifeVision* for this one dimension using the starting exercise of what you wanted to *be, do, and learn.* You developed your *LifeVision* not as a mental exercise, but as an expression of your heart and your deepest desires, and you filled it with emotional content.

5. In this chapter, you've reviewed your vision to identify the characteristics it contains, and you've isolated these in a list that will be a succinct reminder of all you wrote.

6. You finished by brainstorming ideas that would enable you to close the gap between where you are today and making at least one characteristic a consistent aspect of who you are.

That's it so far. Simple, isn't it?

There's one more important aspect of the work you've done so far that I want you to understand. When you identify the characteristics that define you in a particular *LifeDimension,* what you've really done is **establish the standard by which you will live.** Just knowing that your personal standard as a leader includes *Authenticity,* for example, will keep you focused on actions that enable you to live up to this standard. In the same way, establishing that the characteristics of *Thoughtful,* or *Patient,* are part of your personal standard as a spouse or a parent, changes the way you make decisions, as well as the way you react to various situations in your life.

Once you've set the standard, *you can never go back.* As soon as you know that this is who you want to be — that these characteristics represent exactly what you want from your life—each choice you make that is aligned with them will bring you peace and a deep sense of fulfillment. In the same way, each choice you make that is inconsistent with this standard will feel wrong and will drain you of your passion and energy. Having this standard, and the inner knowledge of what it means, will be the compass that keeps your life on track.

***

I know from the many workshops I've taught that this process can already seem like a lot of work. If it does, consider this: if you did every exercise in every chapter so far, you would still have invested less time and energy than the first two days of a college class or the first two days of a new job. From that perspective, it's not really much, is it?

If you're struggling with the time involved in thinking this deeply about your life, then tonight, I want you to try an exercise that will help you stay motivated to create the life you want.

When you climb into bed and finally ease your head toward your pillow, imagine that a simple question is whispered in your ear: *Was today what you wanted?*

Before you fall asleep, be quiet and listen. Your heart will give you a true answer. For many, the painful answer will be no. A few will know the joy of saying yes.

That is why this work is so important: to enable you, from the heart, to answer confidently, *Yes!* And to know that you are truly creating your own extraordinary life.

WHAT ARE YOU PREPARED TO DO?

Move from imagining the life you want to actually living it

Do you know the difference between a fantasy and a vision? Most people don't because both fantasy and vision involve imagining who you want to be and what you want to do. But the difference is as profound and as simple as this: a vision is real and a fantasy is not. What separates them is the answer to a single life-changing question: *What are you prepared to do?*

Many people believe they have a vision for their career, their marriage, or their dimension as a parent or a friend. But because they never follow through on the actions required to fulfill their vision, they reduce it to nothing more than a fantasy. And believe me, a fantasy is worth nothing. At the end of your life, you will find no joy in all that you meant to do, but didn't.

The people who lead great lives, who challenge and inspire us to be like them, are the people who actually do something to make their visions a reality.

There are three key distinctions between a fantasy and a vision that can move you from imagining the life you want to live, to actually living it.

The first distinction is Clarity. In the preceding chapters, you've worked on answering the questions *Who are you?* and *What do you really want?* Through the exercises you've completed, you have begun to do what so few people ever take the time to do: thoughtfully and specifically define what you want from your life. Before now you may have had a fantasy of all you wanted, but you lacked the clarity that comes from putting it in writing.

Remember this: if you're creating a vision for your life and you want it to be real, write it down. It wasn't until I took the time to write all that I would want my children to be able to say about me, that I went from hoping to be a great dad to actually being one.

The second distinction is Progression. Almost nothing of significance can be completed in a single step. In business, you may be familiar with breaking large projects into smaller goals or milestones, but you seldom apply this to your life. This is the work you began in the last chapter by breaking your vision down into characteristics, and then further breaking the characteristics down into ideas for action.

My vision of being a great dad includes a characteristic I call *Adventurous,* which involves spending quality time with my son, Scott, and my daughter, Sarah. An action I take to make this characteristic part of who I am is taking wilderness adventures with them. So, for this year, I've set a goal of taking an eight-day trip with them rafting and kayaking the Middle Fork of the Salmon River in Idaho.

Last year the things I did to embody this characteristic were different, as they will be next year. But over the course of a lifetime, the cumulative effect of these actions has built a great relationship and enabled me to become the dad I wanted to be.

The third distinction is Regular Investment. Even though I've chosen my goals for this year, I still must take the time to plan what to do each week.

Every Sunday for the past twenty-five years, I've spent a few minutes choosing actions that will take me toward my vision in the coming week. In the world of investments, this is known as the *drip* method. Alone, each weekly action might seem insignificant, but cumulatively, they add up to something great.

So, if part of my vision to be a great dad includes taking a phenomenal river trip this year, then my investment toward that goal for this week might be simply to research various guides for the Salmon River, or to buy a map. By reducing this big goal to small, weekly investments, I can make steady progress while still balancing all my other responsibilities.

What are your fantasies? Do you want to be a great leader? A loving and engaged spouse or parent? A trusted and dependable friend? Fit and healthy?

Whatever it is you want from your life, whatever dreams have filled the pages of your *LifeVision,* it will not happen until you determine what you are prepared to do, and then do it. Your fantasy can be transformed into a vision-filled life by simply deciding today to take action. And that's exactly what you will focus on next.

To begin, you need the three things you've already developed: your *LifeVision* for the dimension you most want to work on, a list of the characteristics that vision includes, and your brainstorming ideas on actions that would enable you to become the person those characteristics portray. These are the building blocks for your *LifePlan* in this area of your life.

I'll use the dimension of *Scott and Sarah's Dad* to illustrate how you can develop a plan for a specific area; a plan that will enable you to move from having a vision to actually becoming the person you want to be.

In the *LifeVision* I wrote for being *Scott and Sarah's Dad*, I've distilled a number of characteristics. Here are a few of them:

Always There
Fun
Openhearted
Giving
Accepting
Adventurous
Cool

As much as I want my vision of being a great dad to come true, and as much as I want these specific characteristics to define the dad that I am, I know that nothing will happen without action. So, each year on my birthday, I take the time to reconnect with my vision by reading it again, updating it where it's needed, and feeling the deep emotion that those words have for me. Then, with my vision fresh in my mind, I set one or two major goals for the coming year that will take me closer to seeing that vision become a reality.

Limiting my goals to no more than two ensures that I will be truly focused on them. It also leaves room for other goals that are connected to the remaining dimensions in my life. But most importantly, it forces me to think creatively about what goal will embody the greatest number of the characteristics I want to work on.

I know that my goal of a major river trip will be one way that I can live out the characteristics of spending time with my kids (*Adventurous*), having great laughs (*Fun*), treating them like adults (*Accepting*), listening to them (*Openhearted*)—especially in late-night talks around the

33

campfire—and hopefully, being *Cool* by not flipping my kayak more than once each day.

Not all of my goals are this large. For example, when a career opportunity led Scott to relocate almost three thousand miles away, I set a goal for that year of connecting with him at least once every week. Sometimes we would talk on the phone, and sometimes I would send him a card or an e-mail. But for that year, the characteristic of *Always There* was a challenge I met by focusing on a smaller goal of weekly contact.

Each week, I make at least one investment toward each goal that I've set to ensure that I stay on track. I write down the investments I plan to make and keep them on a special page in my day planner. Here's a look at my page for this week:

Donna's Husband
Bring home flowers on Friday
Research ideas for anniversary present

Sarah and Scott's Dad
Make reservations for Scott, Sarah, and me for rafting trip
Fix the problem with Sarah's computer on Saturday
Lunch and a movie on Friday afternoon (leave work early)
Check on concert tickets for Friday, September 15th
Send Scott a framed picture of the two of us from the conference

CEO
Finalize sales goals and budget for next year
Prepare for board meeting

Writer/Teacher
Write first draft of my commencement speech for KSU
Complete the first draft of next month's column

Martial Artist
Private sparring lesson with Philip
Attend class Tuesday and Thursday night
Stretch three times

Friend
Schedule lunch with Steve

Write note to Andy

Remember that today, I have a written *LifeVision*, as well as at least one key goal for the year, in every dimension. As a result, every action I plan for the week is intentional, not random. Every action I take enables me to live out my vision and most of my actions relate directly to a major goal.

As you can see, my actions for this week that relate to the trip (*make reservations for the rafting trip*) can easily be accomplished in only a few minutes. In addition, I've also chosen a few other actions for Scott and Sarah that enable me to be the dad I want to be, such as helping with a problematic computer or sending a gift.

By consistently and consciously investing **each week**, the cumulative effect is significant. Over time, even the largest of goals, such as a major trip, can be reached, step by step. But more importantly, it makes the journey of my life rich and rewarding, full of a sense of purpose. It is an *intentional* way of living that keeps the investment of my time and energy aligned with what, for me, is most important.

When I have a few moments of open time, whether at work or at home, I will turn to this list and see what I can complete. Many of the items on my weekly page can be done in less than ten minutes. These small, regular investments are the reason I have been able to succeed in so many dimensions over the course of my life, while keeping them all in balance.

Now, it's time to start building your plan for the *LifeDimension* you have chosen. The form is available in the Appendix at the end of this book, as well as on my web site at www.JimHuling.com/forms, and is titled *What I Am Prepared to Do*. This form outlines the major elements you will need to create.

Set a Major Goal for the Year

First, you need to define your goal. Since you are just beginning to use this process, I highly encourage you to choose a goal that is both realistic and meaningful. Otherwise, you may be setting yourself up to fail. Choose a goal that represents a balance between your desire to do something great and the reality of what you will actually follow through on.

If you have a quick temper and a lifetime of explosive reactions, then a goal of becoming completely calm and centered no matter what happens is probably unrealistic for you right now. A more realistic goal would be to begin to pause five seconds before reacting, or to spend thoughtful time understanding the underlying cause of your anger.

My trip down the Salmon River is a big goal, and it is only possible because Scott, Sarah, and I have already taken dozens of trips on similar rivers in the past and have even completed raft guide training. If we didn't have this experience, I would begin with a smaller goal such as completing a paddling class or rafting a smaller river on a day trip.

Setting your goals is also a great time to be creative, rather than analytical. Have fun with it. In the end, you want to choose goals that inspire you, rather than ones where you are worried about how you'll ever do them. Start with something small, such as taking responsibility for planning an evening out with your spouse every other week, to be sure you will succeed. You can always set larger goals when you've accomplished these.

Decide How You Will Keep Score

The second aspect of setting the goal is to determine how you will keep score. This will be one of the most powerful tools in your process, because it enables you to hold yourself accountable for actually doing what you said you would do.

For whatever goal you've chosen, you now need to create a method of tracking your results. For example, I have a master list of everything that's required for our upcoming river trip and each week, when I complete one or two actions that are on that list, I cross them off. I've already reached the point where more than half of the items are crossed off. This simple method is visible evidence that I am making progress that encourages me every time I review it.

For other goals, I might keep score by noting on a separate page each time I did something, or didn't do something, depending on my focus. If one of my goals as a martial artist was to improve my technique this year, I might track my practice sessions. If losing weight was my goal, I would record my weight on the same day each week.

Human beings are oriented to keep score, and when you do, you take the activity more seriously. Most importantly, keeping score enables you to step up your efforts when you're falling behind, and celebrate when you're ahead. When you reach your goal, you will most likely feel that keeping score was your most valuable tool.

Hold Yourself Accountable

Have you ever started a new diet with a goal of eliminating junk food and losing weight? Most of us have at one time or another.

If no one else knows that today is the first day of your new program, then when the candy machine starts whispering your name around 3:00 p.m. it's not a difficult choice to just drop in your money and pull the lever. But if you've told everyone around you *today is the day!* it's very difficult, isn't it? The difference is in the level of accountability you place on yourself.

If there were a giant scoreboard beside a busy highway that displayed all your goals for the year and your results so far, you'd have the ultimate in accountability. You'd also have too much pressure, but you can see how powerful your motivation would be to reach your goals if you knew people were reading your personal scoreboard on their commute every day.

I'm not advocating the giant scoreboard, but I am suggesting you find a way to use accountability to help you stay on track. You might choose to share all your goals with a close friend or with your spouse. Or you might share only the goals that relate to a particular person in one of your *LifeDimensions*. The choice is up to you. But remember, accountability is a powerful force, one that can give you the extra drive you may need during difficult times on the journey to fulfilling your vision. Use it to your advantage.

Whatever method you choose, write down exactly how you will hold yourself accountable on this particular goal.

Plan to Stay Engaged

Inevitably, you will reach a point in the journey toward your goal where you will be tired, under pressure in other areas, or where your inspiration for all you wanted to do simply lags. When this happens, as it does to all of us, you will need to reach for those resources that can help you.

Have you ever listened to the routine speech the flight attendant gives just before takeoff: *In the event the cabin loses pressure, oxygen masks will drop down from overhead.*

Remember what you are supposed to do next? *Put your own mask on first.* Taking care of your own oxygen will enable you to then help others. The same idea is true in the journey of reaching a goal.

The moment when you are facing a crisis or a deep loss of motivation is the worst possible moment to try to think creatively about resources that could help. It is far better to plan now, while the oxygen is flowing, about what you will want to do. There is an ancient teaching that says, *Dig your well before you're thirsty,* and it is great advice for planning ahead for those times when you're down.

When your motivation lags, you might want to call a close friend who has committed in advance to remind you of all the reasons you can, and will, be successful. I have a folder in my desk of special letters, cards, and e-mails that I have received over the years about my leadership ability and my impact on the people around me. When I encounter a moment of self-doubt, I can always take out that folder and begin reading. In only a few minutes, I can feel my spirits lift and I'm ready to get back in the game.

Think now about those resources and people who will help you most in your difficult moments and write them down in the space provided on the form. Then, when the moment hits, you won't have to think about what to do. You can simply follow your own plan for oxygen.

When you've completed the exercises in this chapter, you're ready to begin the journey toward all you've dreamed of in this dimension of your life. It's quite an accomplishment and one that should make you feel very proud.

***

Let's recap the entire process one last time to be sure it's clear.

1. You've defined **Who You Are** by identifying the *LifeDimensions* that make up the life you want to live.

2. For at least one dimension, you've discovered **What You Really Want** by creating a passionate, heart-felt *LifeVision*, including a summary in terms of characteristics.

3. You then decided **What You Are Prepared to Do** by creating the beginning of your *LifePlan*. This included setting goals to enable you to live out the characteristics you want through consistent weekly investments, while keeping score, holding yourself accountable, and staying engaged.

Remember, this is only the beginning. If you were graduating, you would speak of this moment as a commencement, because all you've really done is prepare to live in a different way, a way that now includes a clear understanding of who you are and what you want. It's up to you to make choices, to take action, and to make living according to your vision the most important thing you've ever done, because it is.

I encourage you to begin by staying focused on the goals you have set in the one *LifeDimension* that you used for all the exercises. Work your *muscles* and gain some confidence that you will actually do what you said you would do. Practice keeping score and holding yourself accountable. In other words, work the process for a little while, using the goals you've set in this particular dimension, before you begin to tackle the others in your life.

Then, when you're ready, go back and choose another *LifeDimension*. Proceed through each of the same exercises until you've gained a clear vision of what you want and then set additional goals for yourself.

Take your time. You can't change everything about yourself overnight. Embrace this way of living gradually, but with complete consistency and thoroughness. It won't be long before it is second nature to you and you will see every day the rich rewards of a fulfilling life that will come your way.

PART II
Tools for the Journey

Congratulations! If you've made it this far, then you've done some amazing work defining who you are and what you want from your life. Soon, you should be able to see many positive benefits from your focused and consistent application of the life process contained in Part I of this book (Chapters 1 through 5).

Part II contains a group of important lessons that will also help you on your journey. In this section you'll find everything from how to turn your fear into an ally, to bringing your forgotten dreams back to life.

Each of these lessons is drawn from my personal experience and is told straight from the heart. Think of them as *Traveler's Tips* for your journey. The life process you've already learned is the real map, but each of these additional lessons can have a significant impact on the quality of your results.

Finally, I want to offer you a few closing thoughts on the work you've just begun. Part I of this book outlines a process that represents the cumulative lessons I've learned from a lifetime of excellent teachers, combined with insights gained through personal experience. However, in the end, it is only a process, and a process cannot create a rich, full, and balanced life by itself.

The following thoughts should help to bring it all together and provide my personal *secrets* for making the life you've dreamed of really happen.

1. **It's not real until you schedule it**—You can make all the plans in the world, based on the best theories and practices, but until you *decide* that you will take a specific action, on a specific day, at a specific time, it's not real. What's more, when that day and that time arrive, you must be committed to following through. If you don't, then all the work you've done is just meaningless theory. Each commitment abandoned weakens you. Each commitment kept makes you stronger. Of course, schedules sometimes have to be adjusted and unforeseen circumstances

can overcome even the best intentions. But in the end, actions are all that matter.

2. Shared passions create a multiplier effect—In the beginning, you will think of your *LifeDimensions* individually, as though they were exclusive of each other. However, as you live them out, you will find that many of them can overlap, such that a single goal or weekly action can represent an investment in fulfilling your vision in two or more dimensions. The more you experience this *multiplier effect* (X energy invested = 2X results), the more you start to look for these opportunities, for in them are real leverage and impact.

For example, one of my deepest passions is spending time in the outdoors, hiking, backpacking, and white-water rafting. With the demands on my life, opportunities to be in the wilderness for two or three days are sometimes difficult to make happen. Many years ago, I introduced Scott and Sarah to these outdoor activities and found they shared the same passions. Now, I can take time for something I love, while deepening a relationship with a person I love, using the same investment of time and energy to achieve a greater result (again, X energy invested = 2X results). Sharing the passion also makes every experience more meaningful than it would have been if I had undertaken it alone.

3. Personal values drive the choice of activities—You may have noticed that in Part I, I didn't talk about community service, spirituality, continuous learning, or any number of other topics that are clearly part of leading a full life. For me, these are personal characteristics, not *LifeDimensions*. I use them to drive the types of investments I make in fulfilling each of my *LifeVisions*.

For example, every Christmas, my family and I purchase bicycles for the children in a homeless shelter that we support. For weeks leading up to the actual day when we buy the bikes, I will have planned actions in my dimensions of **Donna's Husband** and **Scott and Sarah's Dad** that involve some aspect of this activity that we will complete together (another example of *shared passion*). In this example, I'm fulfilling a part of my vision for the Dad and Husband I want to be, through one of my characteristics, which is giving to others.

Likewise, my goal to advance as a **Martial Artist** leads me to plan weekly actions of exercising, eating well, and getting adequate rest, thus fulfilling my goals for the year through another of my characteristics: personal health.

Of course, there can be times when a personal characteristic commands a place of such prominence in our lives that it actually becomes a new *LifeDimension* such as **Spiritual Seeker, Community Servant,** etc. However, for me, the dimensions of my life have meant more in terms of relationships and major life responsibilities; personal characteristics have guided the ways in which I have invested in them. Over time, you will find the definition that works for you.

In Part I of this book, and in the special lessons that follow in Part II, you've learned a process for leading an extraordinary life that has worked for me and for the many individuals who have learned it in my workshops. Ultimately, you will need to make this process your own, adding the particular refinements that prove to be most valuable to you through experience. Never forget that this is the work of a lifetime for all of us.

Later, in Part III, you will see how to apply your understanding to your daily life.

I wish you great success and happiness as you learn for yourself that you can create an extraordinary life!

WAKE UP YOUR DREAMS

Use the power of momentum to bring your abandoned dreams to life

D o you remember when you had a truly wonderful dream? A dream so inspiring that it generated an explosive surge of energy every time you thought about it? Perhaps you dreamed of a brilliant career, of being a leader in business, or achieving great financial success. You may have dreamed about the parent or spouse you wanted to be, traveling the world, or developing and expanding your talent for music or art. Like an ocean wave lifting you up, the power of your dream was strong and made you feel you would do anything to achieve it.

What happened to your dream? Where is it now?

In the process of living our lives it's easy to lose our dreams, especially with the pressure of our day-to-day responsibilities. A dream can be like a distant point on the horizon. When you see it through a telescope, it seems so close, and yet when you take the lens away, you realize how far you must go to reach it. Like many, you may have looked across that distance and given up.

I don't have the money.
It'll take forever.
I'm too old to start now.
I'll never find the time.

These are the words of dreams dying. Eventually, you stop dreaming altogether and simply immerse yourself in the demands of your life that are more practical and more urgent. You may rationalize this by reminding yourself that you are a responsible adult with obligations and commitments to fulfill, but in the process, you abandon something vital; something that you will always feel is missing in the life you wanted to create.

Stop for a moment right now and remember your dream. Go back to a time before there were so many concerns and responsibilities, a time when your entire life was still in front of you, stretching out ahead so far that you felt you could literally do anything and you had all the time in the world to do it. Remember?

I believe that you do. When I ask the people in my workshops to raise their hands if they have at least one big dream in their lives that has not come true, every hand goes up. The expressions on their faces are a mixture of nostalgia and pain—pain that, although deeply buried, they are carrying with them every day.

Your dream is still alive. It's inside you right now and every day that you live without pursuing it is a day when you cannot be totally fulfilled or completely at peace. If you will stop long enough to listen to your heart, you will know this is true. And that is what I want you to do now. *Listen to your heart.*

Use the following process, as well as the form provided in the Appendix at the end of the book, or on my web site at www.JimHuling. com/forms, titled *A Dream I Want to Awaken* to guide you in reawakening your dream. As you did with your vision statement in Part I of this book, choose a time when you will not be disturbed, and write the words that come from your heart.

Remember the Dream

You can start by writing, *There was a time in my life when I dreamed of...,* and then let the words flow. Your dream may have been one of *becoming* something, such as a writer, dancer, musician, world-renowned chef, or white-water rafting guide. Or it may have been to *achieve* something, such as backpacking through Europe, hiking the Appalachian Trail, or seeing one of your poems published. The distinction between a *becoming* dream and an *achieving* dream is not important. They are simply two ways of looking at something that you deeply want. What's important is that you reawaken your dream in the language that works for you.

There is a natural resistance to this exercise that almost everyone feels. You may be experiencing it right now. Your inner cynic may be telling you, *This is silly. I don't have time for this. What's the point, anyway?* If so, what you are hearing is simply the voice of fear.

Reawakening a dream can be frightening because it has the potential to disrupt your life, stirring all your old feelings again. You can also fear the pain of remembering something that you truly wanted, but now believe you can't have. These are fears you don't have to face. Your dream can still come true. No matter how unreachable it may seem, you can begin today to move toward it. But first, you must let yourself truly remember it.

Take the time to write everything you once felt and also everything that you can now envision. How did you see yourself being or doing the things you dreamed of? Where did you live, how did you look, and what kinds of clothes did you wear? Were you famous? Did you have freedom to travel, to study, to perform? Were you financially successful? The more vividly you can remember and even expand the dream you once had, the more powerful this exercise will be.

Do it now. Use the form to capture everything you know and remember about your dream.

Brainstorm Ideas for Action

Now it's time to think about what you can do to pursue your dream in even the smallest ways, and within the framework of your current life and responsibilities. The purpose of this section is to generate action ideas, not to evaluate them as good or bad, or to think about where you would find the time or the money. Just start a flow of ideas and get them down on paper.

You can start by writing, *If I were to begin pursuing this dream today, I might...,* and then begin to list actions you could take today. If your dream is to write a book, then your action ideas might be like these:

- *Create three possible titles for my book*
- *Find three books in the bookstore that are similar in content or format to the one I would like to write*
- *Write a two-paragraph overview explaining what my book is about*
- *Find a picture in a magazine or online that illustrates something in my book*

Whatever your dream, use your mind to generate a list of actions that are realistic, achievable, and can be **completed in a single step**. An action item of *Write the book* is useless because it's too large and undefined. You're defeated before you begin it. But very small actions can be easily inserted into your life without disrupting the responsibilities you already carry. They are things you can actually do, not just dream about. The longer you can make this list, the more ideas you will have to work with later and the more your confidence will grow as you see how many things you could really do to begin pursuing your dream today.

Imagine How You Would Feel If You Began to Pursue Your Dream

Take a moment to imagine how you would feel if you really could begin to pursue your dream. See it becoming a part of your life, something that you think about and are pursuing regularly. Envision the day when your small steps have enabled you to finally reach a milestone, something tangible that says you really have become whatever you dreamed of being. See the people around you congratulating you. Feel the confidence, pride, and satisfaction that this moment in your life brings.

Put down the book and close your eyes. Let your imagination run like a film in your mind. *See* it happening, feel your emotions. Let the dream come to life in your mind.

Now commit these thoughts and feelings to paper. Write everything you can, just as you have done with other visioning exercises, but in this exercise specifically envision these things happening now, in the context of your current life. If you want to reawaken your dreams, you must counteract all the times you have conditioned yourself to believe it was impossible to do or be what you dreamed. Seeing your dream happen within a framework that you know is possible will be the antidote to every self-defeating thought you've had, because **every action you've brainstormed could be done today,** not just *someday in the future.*

Harness the Power of Momentum to Make Your Dream Come True

To make your dream begin to come true, you simply need to harness the power of momentum, starting today.

Nowhere is the power of momentum more clearly seen than in the world of sports. How many times have you seen teams ignite an overwhelming victory from a short series of successful plays, or an ice-skater grow more confident with each successful jump? A single stolen ball in a basketball game can completely reverse the momentum, as can a first down or an interception in football. Small successes have real power. They can build the momentum that carries athletes to victory and the same process can work for you. All you need is to be willing to take the first small step.

If your dream is for a different career or a higher level of responsibility, then choose an action item from your list to do **today** such as identifying the skills you will need to be successful. If you've dreamed of writing a book, today create three possible titles. If you've dreamed of being a more engaged parent, today give a small block of undivided attention to your child. Tomorrow you can build on this success by taking another small step, and then another. But tomorrow's success, and the momentum it will carry, will be possible only if you take at least one action today.

I know it's easy to dismiss these small actions as trivial, and instead, do nothing. But, although they may seem insignificant at first, these first steps can be the beginning of something great. Remember, the first person you must convince that you are serious is *you*. Choosing at least one action and following through today literally begins a new dimension to your life. Very quickly, you will feel the power that builds as you see yourself following through on your commitments and making steady progress. Over time, your confidence will grow and one day you will see your dream is starting to come true, even if you've reshaped it to fit into the reality of your life today.

Believe me, you can find fifteen minutes today to take a small step toward your dream.

You spend more time than this discussing the traffic or the latest episode of a popular television show. The return on this investment may be simply the joy of reengaging in something you once loved doing, or it can be a doorway that opens to an entirely new chapter of your life. But whether you are reawakening a dream you once held or creating a new one, nothing will happen until you commit to investing in the first small steps.

Many years ago, I dreamed of being a published writer. Almost three decades later, after two children, three grandchildren, a wonderful marriage, and a great career, I took the first small step toward that dream. And today, you are reading these words.

Achieving your dreams is closer than you might believe.

Do it now. Choose one action from your list and watch what happens when you do it. Then choose another, and another.

Awakening your forgotten dreams is just one way of creating the life you were meant to live. In the next chapter, you'll learn about another— having the courage to be yourself.

HAVE THE COURAGE TO BE YOURSELF

Create the foundation for an authentic life

O K, everyone, it's time to get this deal done," the vice president said proudly to the small group of leaders seated around the boardroom table. "We've been in negotiations for weeks and now it's time to sign the contract."

At that moment, the CEO interrupted him by saying, "Before we sign, I'd like to hear from all leaders that they support this decision."

I saw my entire career flash before my eyes. For weeks, I had been uncomfortable with my required involvement in outsourcing my division. As a mid-level manager, I believed we were doing the wrong thing for all the wrong reasons, but every executive above me advised me to keep quiet and go along. And now, one by one, they were offering the CEO all the reasons this decision was best for the company, reasons I knew they didn't fully believe.

Finally, it was my turn. My heart was racing and my boss was looking directly at me with a clear message in his eyes. It seemed as if the whole world had stopped, waiting for my answer. "I think we should do it," I said, my voice cracking with anxiety. In perfect unison, every person in the room breathed a sigh of relief. And I felt my spirit break.

This moment in my life happened over twenty years ago, but I remember it as if it were yesterday. In choosing to not speak the truth, I traded my integrity for the approval of my boss and then lived through every brutal aspect of the outsourcing with the knowledge that I might have made a difference. This painful experience forged a resolve in me that has become one of the most valuable lessons in my life: the importance of honesty.

Are you honest?

Most likely, you would say that you are and what you usually mean is that you don't intentionally lie. But under the surface, you recognize the temptation that is always there to bend the truth, either to get someone else to sympathize with you or to avoid the conflict that a truly honest answer might create. If you submit to this temptation, you lose a part of yourself and you always know it; it's a sinking feeling that weakens you and makes you want to avoid looking the person in the eyes. Tragically, the people around you know it too. Consciously or unconsciously, they sense that something isn't right and, even if they can't pinpoint it, their trust in you diminishes.

Real honesty is the source of rich relationships and authentic lives— rewards that are worth any sacrifice—but it involves a deeper personal commitment, and to find that level, you must begin to ask yourself tougher questions.

Are You Honest in Everything You Say?

When you relate a story about something that happened at work, do you mix your feelings in with the facts, slanting the story just enough to make your friends or your spouse agree with you? Was the situation exactly as you portrayed it? Or did you bend it a little, just to emphasize how you felt? Are those the exact words your boss used, or are those the words that illustrate how he made you feel? The answers to these questions can help you begin to see where you are being dishonest.

In the beginning, you may get the sympathetic response you want from the person listening to your story, but ultimately it leads them to think you're dishonest. They know it's unlikely to have really happened that way, even if they empathize with how you felt. At some point, they will wonder if you tell stories about them in the same way.

You can start to build relationships of deep trust by clearly separating your feelings from the facts in what you say. Although your feelings about a situation are an important and vital element of what you want to share with another person, be careful that you don't change the story just to illustrate them. It's dishonest to say, *He said I was incompetent,* when what you mean is that he treated you as if you were incompetent. The difference may seem small, but it's a difference that separates the truth from a lie.

Are You Honest When You Are Silent?

More lies are told through silence than through words. Have you ever been part of a group making a tough decision? It may have been your team at work, a parent-teacher organization, or simply a group of friends, but you can probably remember at least once in your life where you disagreed with a group decision, but didn't speak up. Usually, this happens because you want to avoid the disapproval or the controversy that your opinion might create.

In these moments you think, by being silent, you can avoid the conflict and later have no real responsibility for the decision because you never actually said you agreed with them. But you know that this is not really possible. Ultimately, if the group decision was a bad one, those who were in favor of it were simply wrong. But those who only pretended they were in favor were dishonest and risked losing the respect of everyone involved.

Of course, you cannot fight every battle every day, and constantly making your opinion clear to everyone around you will only make you obnoxious. But in the moments that matter, when a real decision is being made or another person really needs to hear a different perspective, you must find the courage to speak up.

When you do, you will generate real respect for yourself and you will earn the respect of others by being clear where you stand on an issue.

Are You Honest in the Image You Project?

Do you have friends or coworkers who believe you respect them, when secretly you don't? It may be that you simply want to avoid hurting them or you might believe they can help your career. But whether kindness or ambition is your motivation, you are actually inflicting a deep wound that will hurt both of you when they learn the truth.

Ultimately, it is fear that drives you to be less than honest about yourself and about what you think and believe—fear that if you let others see you as you really are, they will reject you. Because of this, you construct a false image to get the acceptance you want, but maintaining this false image is both disheartening and exhausting. It requires constant effort, watchfulness, and planning. And in the end, the truth always comes out.

Have the courage to be you. When you have real convictions, state them clearly and factually, giving the people around you the ability to do the same. Honestly sharing your viewpoint, and listening respectfully to the viewpoints of others, not only gives you the freedom to be yourself, it enables everyone to understand the truth of any situation.

Align your actions with what you believe. Consistency creates authenticity and enables others to trust that you are who you appear to be. Ultimately, you need the help and cooperation of the people around you to accomplish anything of significance. Many people will work with you, even if they do not completely agree with your beliefs. But no one will passionately support you if you can't be trusted.

When you set this standard for honesty in everything you say and do, you will discover a new power and confidence within yourself—one that will actually deepen your relationships, strengthen your self-respect, and create the foundation for an authentic life.

In the next chapter, you'll explore the fears that can hold you back and you'll learn a process that will let you face them and become free.

MAKE YOUR FEAR AN ALLY

Learn to know when your fear is helping you and when it's holding you back

I can't do it," I said, as I peered over the edge of the gorge and saw the river, almost 400 feet below. The trail on which we were backpacking had abruptly ended in a sheer drop, continuing only on the other side. Stretched across the gorge was a rope bridge in the shape of a "V," where the bottom rope for my feet was about the size of my wrist, and two smaller ropes, for use as handholds, were placed waist high on either side. "I can't do it," I said more urgently to my uncle, who smiled back at my terrified eleven-year-old face.

"OK," he said, "but before we take the long trail around the gorge, I want you to try something." I didn't know it then, but I was about to learn one of the greatest lessons of my life: how to turn my fear into an ally.

To begin, my uncle asked me to imagine everything bad that could happen if I tried to cross the bridge. It was an easy exercise, since every possible catastrophe was playing through my mind in Technicolor. But as I began to talk about the possibilities, from the rope breaking, to crashing on the rocks below, I sensed a change: I wasn't as afraid as I had been when the thoughts were simply racing through my mind.

When I was only thinking about them, there were many things to fear and each of them seemed very, very large. Saying them out loud made me realize that there were only a few things that I was really afraid of, and when I heard myself say them, I realized how unlikely they were. Forcing my fears out into the light reduced them more than I could have imagined only a few minutes before.

Then he asked me to look across the gorge and describe exactly what it would be like to cross the bridge safely. This exercise was a little harder. But as I began to talk about the feeling of stepping on the bridge, the cool moisture rising up from the river below, the thrill of being suspended in midair, and finally, the exhilaration and pride as my foot touched solid ground on the far side of the gorge, I felt something shift inside me.

"Now," he said, "what do you want to do?"

Without a moment's hesitation, I said, "I want to go across the bridge."

What had changed? I still felt the fear of all that could happen on that bridge, but I had learned to listen to my fears in the context of my hope.

The change this created was much more than just imagining the relief I would have at being on the other side. Instead, it was feeling a deep sense of personal power; power that came from knowing I could face my fears and overcome them. In the end, this is what gave me a sense of personal triumph. The battle had already been fought, and won, inside me. Crossing the bridge was just the result. But the secret that enabled me to overcome my fears was envisioning a successful outcome with the same clarity I had when I imagined falling.

Now, I want you to apply this idea to a fear that you are facing. You can use the form titled *Make Your Fear an Ally* provided in Appendix 1, or available at www.JimHuling.com/forms to get your thoughts down on paper.

State the Situation

You already know what you're facing, but begin to clarify it by writing one or two sentences that describe the exact situation, such as:

My job has become really boring. I haven't felt challenged in months and I'm sure my attitude shows in my performance. But the idea of a new job really frightens me. What will happen if I take another job and then don't like it, or wish I was back here? What if I really can't make it somewhere else?

This is a familiar example, but you could just as easily be facing the uncertainty of a new relationship, moving to a new city, or the illness of a loved one. Although each of these situations is unique, the process of working through your fears is the same.

Bring out Your Fears

Begin to list everything bad that could happen. Don't be an optimist; get it all out on paper in the most vivid, excruciating detail you can imagine. Just be sure everything you list is something you are really afraid of, and that you're not simply writing a script for the next blockbuster horror movie. Be realistic. If you find yourself imagining that a meteor could fall from the sky and crush the building on the first day of your new job, you've gone too far. That same meteor could be headed toward you right now, wherever you are, and you're probably not looking up.

List each fear individually, so you can work on them one by one. Many times, when all those fears are running around in your mind, they are like a ball of snakes twisting, turning, and wrapping around each other. Together, they seem like one giant fear, but when you separate them, you see them as a collection of smaller fears that, individually, aren't so frightening.

Once you've listed each fear, the next step is to assess how likely each one is to actually happen. To do this, place a letter beside each fear to indicate the following:

R—Realistically could happen
U—Unlikely, but possible
N—Never will happen

Each fear you labeled R is something you need to think about and prepare for. For these fears, which are the only ones that deserve a lot of attention, you should ask yourself two questions:

Is there anything I could do now to eliminate this fear or reduce the likelihood of it happening? For example, if your new job involves presenting information to groups of people and you're uncomfortable with speaking, you might want to take a class on public speaking or join an organization such as Toastmasters before you make the change. If this is a major fear for you, then the time and investment you will make to eliminate it will be well worth it.

Am I fully prepared to accept the possibility, and the consequences, if the worst possible outcome happens? Remember, there are no meteors coming your way. But if the new job involves a lot of travel and you have never before endured the rigors of airport delays, lost luggage, and hotel accommodation snafus on a regular basis, then this is an issue that could go very wrong. In this case, you need to assess what you will do if, after a few months, you can't take it anymore.

If you do end up in your worst case scenario, you will still have many options available, such as finding another job outside of, or within, your new company, or talking to your new boss about reducing your travel. But the more important point is: *are you prepared to accept the consequences?* If you're not, then this issue could be a deal breaker and, if it is, your fears about travel have been an early warning sign that you could be making the wrong decision.

Once you've evaluated each of the realistic fears labeled R, you're ready to work with the less impactful ones labeled U. These should be only generally evaluated, using the same approach of determining whether they could be eliminated or accepted. But as you do this, remember that you've assessed them as unlikely to actually happen, so your need to actually work on them should be minimal.

I once had a friend who decided to turn down a job offer because he was afraid that the company making the offer might one day be sold.

"Are they actively trying to sell it now?" I asked him.

"No, but they might," he responded. "They've been growing a lot and they're really successful."

"Are there any plans or even rumors that they might sell one day?" I asked.

"No, but you never know," my friend replied, shaking his head knowingly.

"So, let me get this straight," I said. "What you're really looking for then is a company that is unsuccessful and failing to grow that will promise you they will never be sold?" My friend looked at me as though I'd slapped him.

I couldn't resist adding, "That really sounds a lot like the company you work for now. You must be really happy."

This conversation is funny when it isn't happening to you, but we can all remember a moment when we let a very unlikely fear begin to grow in our minds to the point where it overshadowed everything else. The fears labeled U fall into this category.

My wife, Donna, once taught me a powerful method for dealing with these kinds of fears. It consists of a one-word question: *So?*

No matter how simple it may seem, you'll feel the power when you begin to use it. Take one of the fears in this category, imagine it happening, and then say it out loud. *So?* This one word shifts your mind away from being a victim and toward all the possibilities.

In my friend's example above, I encouraged him to try it with his fear of the new company being sold. After restating his fear, he then said the word: *So?* He paused thoughtfully for a moment, and then began to list all the things he would do, the resources he would tap, and the possibilities that he could envision. In an instant, you could see the change in his face. He knew that if the thing he feared were to happen, he could handle it, and this confidence gave him the power to move forward..

Finish the exercise by simply smiling at all the fears you've labeled N because, like the meteor that *might* crash into your new building, they are fears that, once out on paper, have no ability to affect you.

Envision the Outcome You Want Most

Here's where the fun begins.

Just as you did in the life planning process in Part I, begin to envision all that you want to happen, all that will and can happen, when you face this challenge and succeed. Using our same example of starting a new job, close your eyes and imagine the excitement of your first day, how pleased the new company is that you have joined them, and all the exciting new projects and responsibilities you will have. Think about how well your experience has prepared you for this moment and how much you have to offer.

Experience in your mind what it will feel like to make a fresh new start; one where the mistakes you've made in the past are no longer relevant, and one where everything you've learned will help you create a new future. See yourself looking back one day at all the fears that might have kept you imprisoned in a job you'd outgrown. Feel the self-respect, confidence, and sense of personal power you now have because you chose to overcome them and start this new chapter of your life.

The more vividly you perform this exercise, the more realistically you can make a final decision about whether your fear is helping you or holding you back.

I'm certain some of you will want to dismiss this exercise as *unrealistic* because it asks you to focus only on the positive things that could happen. If this is how you're thinking, then consider this: When you're facing something you're afraid of, are your fears vividly clear in your mind? Do you have a miniature movie running all the time of the things that could go wrong? Of course you do.

But when you think about this fear, do you have an *equally clear picture* of all that could go right? Not often. You usually excuse this by saying, *I'm just being realistic about what could happen.* **But what you're actually doing is weighing fears that are extremely clear against hope that is vague and undefined.**

Would you make any other decision in your life this way? Probably not. And yet, the decisions you fear—those that involve a degree of risk—are usually the ones that matter most.

When you envision all the positive outcomes that could occur with the same clarity as those you fear, you are simply balancing the scale so that your ultimate choice is *more* realistic. You can make the best decisions for your life only through a balanced view such as this. Without this perspective, you will choose to avoid risk and endure stagnation forever.

Make a Choice

Some people listen only to their fears, and for them, the voice of fear is too great, overshadowing every other thought. In this state, they are paralyzed, turning away from every new challenge and opportunity. Others block the voice of their fears completely, refusing to even acknowledge them. This is like running with your eyes closed. You can avoid seeing your fears, but you may also fall into a deep gorge.

You need to listen to your fears, but you must also weigh them against the passion and hope of your outcome. Fear can be a good teacher when it warns you that you are not ready for something. But fear can also be a poor judge of readiness, since it judges only on what you have done before, not on what you are capable of doing for the first time. Ultimately, you must decide whether your fear is helping you or holding you back.

If you use this process to make your fear an ally, you will find each fear to be either a warning enabling you to avoid real danger, or simply the small voice inside all of us that resists the unknown, a voice that you must acknowledge and move beyond if you are to grow and attempt great things.

Are there bridges of your own you need to cross? Overcome your fears and take the first courageous step. The greatest achievements in your extraordinary life are waiting for you.

In the next chapter, you'll focus on using these tools to overcome one of your most basic fears—the fear of change.

OVERCOME YOUR FEAR OF CHANGE

Three decisions that will enable you to triumph over uncertainty

The new owners are changing everything and there are rumors that my entire division will be reorganized," my friend Bob said to me over lunch. "I can't believe this is happening. Why couldn't things have stayed the way they were?"

I know my face showed the astonishment I felt, not over the changes in his company, but over the change in Bob. For as long as he had worked there, Bob had been the resident expert on all that was wrong in the organization, from poor management and shifting priorities, to the quality of the food in the cafeteria. And now he was upset that things were finally changing.

What had happened?

In facing one of the most significant changes of his life, Bob had become so afraid of what might happen that he actually preferred his negative current situation over an uncertain future. His fear made him unable to see that this change might create the very outcome he had wanted for years.

Fear is always at the heart of our resistance to change. Like Bob, it's not really the changes you fear; what you fear is their uncertainty. One of the greatest lessons you can ever learn in life is that *you have the power to choose how you deal with uncertainty.*

If you are faced with the uncertainty of change in any area of your life, remember that there are three decisions you will inevitably make. The decisions are not optional—you *will* make them—but what you choose will always be up to you.

You Will Decide What You Are Going to Focus on

You already know that every change has the possibility of either a positive or a negative outcome. For example, the organizational change at your company that might eliminate your job could also create the opportunity for a promotion or align you with a new leader who will become your greatest mentor.

Often, both outcomes are equally likely. But which one do you usually focus on? My friend Bob not only focused on the worst, he envisioned a bad outcome in such vivid detail that he became almost certain it would happen. This imagined outcome was so real to him that it affected his health, his performance at work, and ultimately his relationships at home. At a time when he needed his best performance, all his energy, and the full support of his family, he chose a focus that robbed him of all three.

Why not decide to focus your mind more broadly on all the possibilities and consistently envision something good coming from them? No matter what actually happens, choosing this mindset every day will channel your fear of uncertainty into the kind of attitude and performance that create opportunity.

You Will Decide What You Are Prepared To Do

Change forces choices. Whether you have to take on expanded responsibilities, learn a new skill, or adapt to a new boss, times of change don't allow you to stand still. Each new demand forces you to decide what you are willing to do.

But how can you make these decisions if you don't know what you want?

Use this time to make a new plan for your career and for the life you want using the life planning process described in Part I of this book. Without a plan, every new demand is just more work. But if you know where you want to go, you could find that the new skill you are being forced to learn actually moves you closer to your dream job for the future.

You Will Decide Who You Will Become

No matter what changes you are facing, the most important change is happening inside you. Are you becoming bitter and angry or are you seeing the hopeful possibilities and encouraging the people around you? Are you becoming inflexible and difficult or are you stretching out of your comfort zone and learning new things?

Take a hard look at yourself. **Others may have created the changes you face, but you are choosing who you become because of them.**

Change is inevitable. But based on the decisions you make, it can be a resentful struggle or it can be a time when you learn your most valuable lessons, discover inner strength and capacity, and reveal who you really are.

The choice is up to you. What may surprise you is that there is a part of you that already knows the answer. In the next chapter, you'll learn to listen to your inner voice, the one that knows best who you really are.

LISTEN TO YOUR OWN VOICE

Stay true to yourself and you will never be lost

Have you ever been really lost? Even for a moment, have you been unsure of where you were or which way to go? Do you remember the feeling? The anxious, almost panicked urgency that made you want to walk faster, or run, or drive—anything to be headed back to familiar territory and away from that dark cloud of helplessness that rises when you don't know where you are.

People who are lost usually run faster in the wrong direction. Every frantic step takes you farther away from where you wanted to be and heartbreakingly farther from any chance of help.

There are so many ways to become lost. When you're asked to do something that will enhance your career but compromise your personal integrity, you can feel lost in an ocean of rationalizations and imagined consequences. Your mind processes the different things you could do or say, always searching for a way to balance what you've been asked to do with what you know is right, while minimizing your risk. But in the end, this only leaves you more confused.

When you know that a friend desperately needs to hear a painful truth, but telling that truth may damage the friendship, you can feel lost in all the reasons why you shouldn't say what needs to be said.

Like a person lost in the woods, you begin to run in the wrong direction.

You avoid the situation or the person, hoping that the choice will go away. You ask advice from everyone who will listen, secretly wishing he or she would make the decision for you. You rationalize endlessly, trying to find some emotional algebra that will make doing the wrong thing the right choice. The more you run, the farther you are from knowing what to do.

Finding Your Way Home

In an earlier time, when becoming lost was literally a matter of life and death, the Native Americans passed an ancient teaching to their children: *When you are lost, stand still. Remember that the trees are not lost, they are home. Come to know the place, and you will be home too.*

Even in the very different worlds of business, career, family, and friendships, this teaching can still help you find your way home.

Do you feel lost today in a forest of conflicting priorities, pressures to compromise your values, or uncertainty about what really matters to you? Have you been asked to do something at work that doesn't seem right? Sometimes the pressure to bill the extra hours, tell the customers what they want to hear, or stay silent when you should speak up can be enormous.

Are you lost in a relationship that seemed so right in the beginning, but is now tangled in layers of anger, resentment, or apathy? Over time, your patterns of action and response can become so ingrained with another person that they are automatic. Finding again the core passion and love that you once felt can seem impossible, leaving you lost between the choice of abandoning the relationship or working to save it.

When your mind is racing and your emotions are high, you panic. And in that state, you begin to ask yourself all the wrong questions. *What will happen if I say no? Will it cost me my job or my relationship? What went wrong? Why is this happening to me?*

None of these questions will lead you to the answer you need, because they are questions directed at your mind, as though the answer you need could be found through enough data and analysis. Although your mind is a powerful tool, it's almost useless in situations like this.

If this is where you are, then stop. Stand still. And listen. Find a quiet place and ask yourself a simple, but powerful question: *What is the right thing to do?* I promise you, the answer will come.

Listen to Your Inner Voice

Even in the most difficult circumstances, if you stop long enough to hear your inner voice, you will find you were never really lost. You will realize you always knew the right thing to do; you were simply frightened of doing it.

You see, living a great life is not really about achievement, financial success, or any of the other surface-level ways in which you measure. It's about being true to who you really are, about living in such a way that your actions are aligned with what you believe.

If you make decisions based on what you think will get you the raise, make others like you, or any other artificial reason, you become separated from your true self. That's when you feel lost. And losing yourself is always the greatest tragedy.

The decisions that matter most in your life are meant to be answered from the heart. If you listen closely, and then have the courage to act on what you know is right, you will never be lost.

Wherever you are, remaining true to yourself will show you the way. And once you know it, you only need to begin. In the next chapter, you'll learn how to take that courageous first step.

TAKE A COURAGEOUS FIRST STEP

Focus on the end to unleash your confidence to begin

I stood barefoot before the glowing bed of coals whose temperature had been measured at almost two thousand degrees. For the past six hours I had been preparing for this moment, focusing my mind on a single objective: to cross the fourteen feet of burning coals without injury or pain. I believed I was ready, but now, with the heat rising up to sting my face, I was hesitating. Doubts began to flicker across my mind as I tried to maintain my concentration.

You're too old to do this.
Maybe you should wait.
You're not ready yet.

I almost walked away. Then, I heard the quiet, steady voice of my teacher speaking in my ear. He gave me a simple, but profound instruction that has become one of my greatest lessons: Focus on the end. Have faith. Take the first step.

Are you facing a moment of decision? As you envision the year ahead, is there something you've been waiting to do, something you know would take your life to the next level of success and fulfillment, but now you are hesitating?

If so, your challenge is not in knowing what you want; it's in taking action to make it a reality. As I was in the moment before my fire walk, you can be tempted to wait, postponing your dreams for another day.

You may be telling yourself that the time is not right or that you need more preparation, or even worse, that your chance to be or do what you've dreamed of has passed you by. These are the lies that fear whispers in the moment of decision, and if you listen to them they will keep you from beginning.

Focus on the End

Think for a moment of the most significant things you've accomplished so far in your life, whether it's rising to a certain level in your career, mastering a special skill, or nurturing and guiding your children through the years.

Although you succeeded in the end, each of these accomplishments involved thousands of hours of effort, required you to adapt for unexpected challenges and included the painful lessons of failure along the way. If you had focused on all of this effort and challenge in the beginning, you might never have begun.

Instead of thinking about all that your new goal will require of you, focus on the end, on all that you want. Develop a compelling vision and then hold a clear and vivid image of the deep satisfaction you will feel when you've accomplished the goal. Focusing on the end will give you the energy and confidence to begin.

Have Faith

In each of the accomplishments you just thought about, was there a single one that you were completely prepared for when you began? Was there one where you had already mastered the skills, had the experience, or didn't have to adapt to things you would never have expected? Of course not, because what makes these accomplishments so meaningful is how much you grew in the process of achieving them.

Understanding how far you've come strengthens your faith in where you can go. As you face your new goal, know that you will again be guided in each step along the way, that you will again grow and develop and, most importantly, that you will persevere.

Have faith in yourself and in all you believe, and you will have the courage to begin.

Take the First Step

Ultimately, everything you want comes down to your willingness to take the first step. All that you have accomplished so far, and all the joy and fulfillment it has brought, was only possible because there was a moment when you finally began to move forward.

My first step crossing the burning coals, and the intense heat all around me, is all I really remember before I arrived on the other side, unharmed. But the joy of that accomplishment, and the inner strength it created, has changed me forever.

When you finally realize that all the possibilities of your life are waiting for you to take the first step, you will have the strength to begin. Once you do, you open the floodgates of possibility.

In the next chapter, you'll learn about a powerful tool that can either hold you back from the life you want, or can enable you to confidently step forward—the power of your inner dialog.

CONTROL YOUR INNER DIALOG

Use the power of your thoughts to open a floodgate of energy

D o you remember the first thought you had today? Perhaps it was something like this: *I'm worried about that project. The meeting we've scheduled probably won't go well. I've never been good at solving problems.*

With these first thoughts, you began an inner dialog that will repeat continuously throughout the day.

Before long, you'll expand this dialog to include your concern for the tragedies you heard on the morning news, your anger at the inconsiderate drivers on the road, and resentment of the boss who doesn't appreciate you. By midday this stream of unconscious negative messages will be in full force, shaping the way you see the people and circumstances of your life. And because it's so familiar, you may be unaware that the dialog even exists.

When you allow these thoughts to dominate your mind, it's like someone standing behind you throughout the day, whispering into your ear, *This is not going well. You can't trust anyone. You've failed before and you'll probably fail again.*

Your mind accepts this endless repetition of negative thoughts as reality, and this acceptance actually creates a negative perspective on your life, undermines your confidence, and diminishes your hope. Most importantly, these thoughts can drain the energy you need to create the life you want.

What if today, you decided to think differently?

My wonderful wife, Donna, once taught me that a miracle can be as simple as a change in perspective. And this is what happens when you begin to take control of your inner dialog as one of the most important tools in life: a change in your perspective emerges that can open a floodgate of energy.

Begin with Gratitude

You can begin right now by filling your mind with gratitude. Think about the aspects of your life for which you are grateful and say them aloud with real passion: *I'm grateful for another day. I'm grateful for my family, for my health, and the love that enriches my life. I'm grateful for my work and the income it provides...*

Could you feel the difference? Even if you were skeptical, did you sense your energy lift as you expressed your gratitude again and again?

Now think about a specific challenge you are concerned about at work, one where there are consequences if you fail and no easy answers in sight, and say the following phrases several times: *I can do this. I have the talent and the experience I need to be successful. This is going to turn out well.*

Did you feel a shift in your perspective?

When you approach a challenge by keeping your thoughts focused on a positive outcome, you generate the energy and confidence you need to be successful, instead of constantly undermining yourself. In the end, you will not only deliver a better result, your entire experience of working on the challenge will be transformed.

Use Your Thoughts to Transform Your Relationships

What about your relationships outside of work? Do you have a friend or family member who is causing you concern? Examine your inner dialog about the person and you may hear something like this: *He never takes responsibility for his actions. Everything he does turns out badly. I'm always afraid for him.*

Changing your inner dialog about another person can also have a truly transformative effect. Replace your negative thoughts with a positive acknowledgement of some aspect of the person, such as: *Each of his choices is teaching him a valuable lesson. I know he's capable of changing. I believe in him.*

You'll be surprised at what happens to both of you. Your positive focus will not only shape your perspective, it will give the other person the empowering gift of your belief and confidence in him.

Finally, remember that whether positive or negative, your inner dialog is unstoppable. It continuously shapes your perspective on every aspect of your life. Only you have the power to choose the content of that dialog.

By choosing thoughts that empower you and the people around you, you will create a powerful shift in perspective, a shift that will generate newfound energy in you and in everyone you meet.

In the next chapter, you'll meet Ezekiel, a man who has clearly chosen to think, and live by, empowering thoughts. My encounter with him gave me a living example of the power of kindness, both as a way of living and of changing the world.

ACT WITH CONSCIOUS KINDNESS

Make the defining choices that have a profound impact

I was already late when the shuttle bus stopped outside the airport and I realized suddenly that I had forgotten to lock my car. There were valuable items in the car that I did not want to risk losing, but there was no time for the trip back to the parking facility without missing my flight. If you've ever been in a situation like this you won't be surprised that I was stressed and frustrated. As the other passengers began to grab their bags and step off the bus, I sat in my seat with no idea what to do.

"Is there anything I can do to help?" the bus driver named Ezekiel asked, sensing my distress. There was something in the sound of his voice that slowed the whirlwind of thoughts racing through my mind. He seemed so calm and genuinely interested in helping me that it took me by surprise, especially on a bus filled with passengers anxious to get to their flights.

When I explained the situation, he simply smiled, wrote down the space number where I had parked my car, and promised to lock it when he returned to the facility, assuring me that my keys would be waiting at the front desk. I offered to pay him, reaching for my wallet, but he refused. He looked me directly in the eyes and said, "I'm happy to do it." His response was so genuine that I could only shake his hand before I rushed into the airport filled with relief and gratitude at this unexpected act of kindness from a stranger.

I know you could easily say this is just a story of good customer service. Perhaps all the employees of the parking facility were trained to do the same thing for customers in similar circumstances. But I doubt it. I believe Ezekiel's response was the result of a personal choice, a choice to act with conscious kindness.

There were many other passengers on the bus that morning waiting to be shuttled to other airlines. He was under pressure to hurry on and yet, Ezekiel chose to stop and offer kindness to a stranger who seemed troubled. It was a choice that had a profound impact on me beyond simply relieving my anxiety over my car. It taught me again the power of kindness.

The Power of Kindness Ripples Outward

A short time later, I was at the security checkpoint behind a woman traveling with two small children. The line had completely stopped moving as she struggled to carry one child and herd another through the process of removing shoes and belts. As quickly as she focused on one child, negotiating to place a beloved doll in the plastic tray for security scanning, the other would start to put her shoes back on. It was a scene that is not uncommon in airports today, as harried mothers attempt to travel with children.

"Oh, great. This is all I need," said a man behind me in an angry voice. He dropped his briefcase with a loud and symbolic thud on the airport floor, crossed his arms over his chest, and began railing about how important his trip was to closing a big deal. Everyone in line could hear him, including this struggling mother. In an instant, I realized that the look of distress and anxiety on this woman's face must be the same look Ezekiel had seen on mine earlier that morning.

"Is there anything I can do to help?" I asked, handing her two of the plastic trays used for personal items and setting my own briefcase down to free my hands.

"Would you?" she said, giving me a diaper bag and her purse.

"I'm happy to do it," I said, as she filled the trays with toys, shoes and her toddler's pink backpack, while I placed her purse and diaper bag on the conveyer belt. As she guided the children through the metal detector, she glanced back at me with a smile of gratitude clear on her face, and it gave me a feeling of real joy.

Sometimes in the hurry of life you can be so focused on yourself that you think your needs are the only ones that matter. You become angry and impatient at anyone, or anything, that hinders you. When the car in front of you drives too slowly or you have to wait for a cashier to check the price of an item, you respond in ways that later make you feel regretful or even ashamed.

The business traveler who became angry and hurtful to this mother is probably not a bad person. He is simply a person who made a bad choice. And when it comes to the tiny moment between an event and your response to the event, you must remember that you, too, always have a choice.

Your Choices Define Who You Are

Sometime soon, if not today, you will be under stress. A deadline may be looming and one of the people you work with may fail to carry his or her share of the workload. Computers may crash, messages may be lost or inaccurately relayed, or your important meeting may be interrupted by an unexpected fire drill in your building. There are hundreds of possibilities, but the event itself doesn't really matter. What matters is how you respond.

These types of events happen to everyone and are so common they are often referred to as *just life*. How you respond is much more specific. It's called *you*, because ultimately, *these are the choices that define who you are.*

When frustrations occur, you can choose to be angry and more demanding of the people around you, or you can remember that they, too, are under similar stress and you can offer to help them. The choice is yours, but it's a choice that will be remembered, especially in difficult moments.

If your habitual response to stress at work is to make everyone miserable, then you must accept responsibility for two outcomes that are inevitable.

First, you make the people who have to work with you less productive, not more. You may momentarily satisfy your own need to express frustration or anger, but you will increase theirs, and the result will be work that is done grudgingly and with no real passion.

Second, you are defining your own identity, an identity that will be reinforced as the story of your behavior is told over and over again by the people you work with, whether at their family dinner table, a neighborhood gathering, or the weekend ball game. Eventually, it becomes the truth of who you are; a truth that is so widely known, it is accepted by everyone.

Imagine if one day, the business traveler who was cruel to the mother in line, came to be interviewed by me for a job. Most likely, he wouldn't even remember his actions on that day. But I would. The principle of karma is always in effect: what you sow is truly what you reap. Without realizing why, he would face a huge challenge in convincing me that he should join my company because of the person his actions revealed him to be that day in line.

The same frustrations, and the same choices, can happen just as easily in your relationships with your family or friends. When they do, you can choose to lash out, saying things that you will later regret, or you can stop to remember that these are the people you care most about and you can choose to treat them with patience and love.

In your final moments of life, when the day-to-day concerns that fill your mind today become unimportant in the context of what really matters, these are the choices you will wish you had made. Why not make them now?

Each choice you make to show kindness to another person ripples outward from that person to another, beyond your imagination. Ezekiel's kindness to me shifted my entire perspective. A day that could have been one of my worst, with either a missed flight or a vandalized car, became a day that changed me. His kindness then rippled outward from me to the mother in need of help, and beyond, in a force that is probably still going today. I am completely certain that, one day, it will also return to him in some way.

Later, I was finishing a cup of coffee while waiting to board the plane when I heard someone say, "Excuse me, sir. I believe you dropped this." A woman was calling out after a man hurriedly rolling his bag toward the check-in counter. It was the mother I had helped earlier.

She handed him a small plastic card that I could see was his driver's license. For a moment, he was speechless.

"Thank you so much," he then said, grasping the enormous difficulty he would have faced in attempting to travel without it.

"I'm happy to do it," was all I heard her say as I entered the gate to walk onto the plane.

Somehow, I knew Ezekiel was smiling. To this day he remains one of my heroes because of the lesson he taught me.

In essence, kindness is a powerful way you give yourself to the people in your life. So is giving them the gift of your trust. In the next chapter, you'll learn the power, and the importance, of choosing whom to trust with the things that matter most.

KNOW WHOM TO TRUST

Ask the deeper questions that determine trustworthiness

O n belay?" I called out the rock climber's command for readiness
as I scanned the rock face for my first foothold. "Belay is on!"
said my daughter, Sarah, who was only thirteen years old at the
time.

Something about the sound of her voice made me turn to her. When
I did, I saw the look of absolute determination on her face, a look that
said, "I've got you, Dad." I began to scale the rock face, knowing that my
life might be in her hands at any point along the 200-foot wall of rock I
was about to climb.

How did I decide to trust Sarah so much, especially at such a young
age? The answer is in knowing how to balance trust and trustworthiness.
It's one of the most important lessons in creating an extraordinary life.

Have you ever placed your trust in the wrong person? Do you
remember how it felt when he or she let you down? Often, the deepest pain
in our lives comes from those moments when our trust was betrayed and
yet, you must trust others in some area of your life almost every day.

So, how do you decide when and whom to trust? You can begin by
realizing that the decision to trust someone involves two questions—one
you usually ask and one you usually forget.

Whether in business or in a relationship, when you decide to trust
someone you evaluate the external factors first. Is he mature enough? Does
she have the skills and experience? Does he seem committed? In essence,
you are asking yourself the first question—*Can* he do it? Certainly, this is
the place to start. A person who does not meet these requirements, at the
level needed to fulfill the responsibility, is not ready to be trusted.

But this is usually not the problem. Most of your disappointments
come from your failure to ask the second, deeper question—*Will* he do it?

If you fall during a climb, your partner instantaneously makes a
pivotal choice: whether to hold the rope or let it slide through his or her

hands. When you think back to the people who have betrayed your trust, you will usually find that they were completely capable of doing what they committed to do, but in the moment of choice, they were simply not willing to do it. In creating your life, you want to depend on people who won't let you fall.

The next time you choose to trust someone, remember that there is a difference between their being capable of fulfilling a commitment and actually following through on it. Real trustworthiness includes both.

Ask yourself the deeper question of what she will do in the moment of choice. Watch how she fulfills her commitments to others in both small and large responsibilities. If she says the report will be done this week, does it happen? If she agrees to meet you at a certain time, is she there? Personal responsibility is like a light switch in most people; it's either on or off. While no one is perfect, if she takes small commitments seriously, she is very likely to make large commitments with the same seriousness.

Remember, also, that others are asking and answering the same questions about you. Do you consistently do what you say you will do? Or do you make promises with the expectation of adjusting them later? Beware of the times that you make a commitment by saying you will try to do it. "Try" is a word that clearly says you are not committed and are already hedging. In essence, it's a way of preparing to fail with honor. Eliminating this one word from your vocabulary, and instead making an absolute commitment to do something, will increase your trustworthiness tenfold.

Halfway up the rock face, my foot slipped and I saw the ground rushing up toward me, only to be interrupted by a violent jerk as the rope broke my fall, leaving me safely suspended in midair. I looked down to see Sarah holding on to the rope with all her might. I had chosen the right person to trust.

Who's holding your rope today? Can he or she be trusted? Can you?

One of the most powerful ways that we enable others to trust us is by having the courage to be vulnerable. In a world that seems to value only perfection, vulnerability about our weaknesses and the things we fear is becoming more and more rare. In the next chapter, you'll learn about the power and the strength that can be found in true vulnerability.

FIND STRENGTH IN YOUR VULNERABILITY

Create a connection that builds trust and respect

I stood before my company in what I knew would be a defining moment. After a decade of phenomenal success, the market had turned, sharply and unexpectedly. The financial impact was devastating. Difficult decisions had to be made that included layoffs, expense reductions, and the plotting of a new strategy for the future. All of this would be painful, and a fearful uncertainty overshadowed my entire team. As I walked to the podium, their faces showed the same concerns that I felt churning inside me.

In that moment, I had two choices in what I would say. One choice was to be vulnerable, to let them see that I felt the same emotions and the same regret they did over the issues we faced, and to then use that connection to take us forward together. The other choice was to act as though I had everything under control, displaying confidence that in my heart, I did not feel. Unfortunately, this was the one I chose.

The message I gave could best be characterized as a *pep rally* speech, with lots of bravado that I now know seemed as false to them as it did to me. I concluded by stepping off the stage and shouting, "Let's make it happen!" After a brief moment of forced applause, they quietly left the room having gained no hope or courage from my attempt at a rallying message.

Even today, I still cringe at this memory. And yet, this experience taught me one of the greatest lessons in choosing your life.

Are you facing a challenge today that has you feeling overwhelmed or frightened, unsure what to do?

Whether you are a leader in business, the coordinator of a community project, or the parent of maturing children, you will inevitably face a moment such as this. And when it happens, you may be tempted to act as though you have it all under control and need little help from anyone else. Take it from me, this is the wrong approach.

It's easy to believe you should have all the answers for every situation. And when you do, you hesitate to ask for help, even when you know you need it. You work to seem confident and assured, when what you should be doing is asking the people around you to join in finding a solution. Imagine if I had begun my meeting by acknowledging that I had been affected by the changes, just as they had, and then asked for ideas on how we could get through the crisis together. Would they have thought less of me as a leader, or more? I think you know the answer. And the same is true in your situation.

When you are willing to let others see that you can have the same doubts, the same fears as they do, it does not make you weak. It makes you human. Courage is not the absence of fear, it is action taken in spite of it. Your willingness to be vulnerable creates a connection that not only *enables* others to help you, it makes them *want* to. The result is unity, in your family or your team, which strengthens everyone and displays the truest form of courage.

Vulnerability also makes you stronger when you've made the wrong decision or said something that you later regret. Instead of defending your actions, acknowledge your mistake and what you've learned from it. Remember that the people around you always see the truth eventually. They can respect you, in spite of your mistake, if you are simply willing to admit it.

I once worked for a leader who, although respected for his passion, thoroughness, and hard work, was widely known for never making two important statements: *I was wrong* and *I'm sorry*. Like everyone, he was sometimes wrong, but staunchly refused to admit it. Because of this, the people on his team became unable to trust him, and eventually, he was removed from his position.

Your vulnerability is what enables you to connect with the people in your life. The more you connect, the more engagement, respect, and trust you will experience. And the more of a leader you will become.

PART III
Choosing Your Life Every Day

Once you understand the questions that really matter and the tools to aid you on your journey, you face the most difficult task of all—choosing every day to live true to your vision of who you are and the life you were born to live. The purpose of this section is to help you in this process.

In the pages that follow you will find real-life stories of how I have applied these lessons to my life, not only to deepen my vision, but also to enrich it. You will also read about the hard-won lessons I've learned along the way in the hope that they will drive home the importance—the true life-altering urgency—of choosing your life in every moment of every day.

As you read them, see yourself applying the lessons they offer to the people and circumstances of your own life. In this way, you can build on the experience of my personal journey in creating the life you want most.

CREATE TREASURED MEMORIES

Make time for your most memorable moments

I stood in the bow of the raft, balancing myself against the turbulence of the water, and said good-bye to the hundred miles of raging white water that had been my home for the past six days. Beside me stood my son, Scott, and my daughter, Sarah, also saying farewell. I saw tears in their eyes that matched my own as I put my arms around them both and knew the memory of these days together would last forever.

As we later huddled together in the small plane that took us over the mountains, I thought about the special memories we shared from this amazing trip: the towering rapid that crashed over my kayak and sent me swimming to the laughter of my children, the talks we had around the campfire after long days of paddling, and the deeply spiritual night we slept at the site of a Native American campground.

It wasn't easy to make time for this trip. My responsibilities at work had never been greater. There were urgent and important issues that seemed to come up every day and when I thought about being away for almost two weeks, I wondered how I could possibly do it. Being completely unreachable—no cell phone, BlackBerry, or wireless Internet—only compounded my concerns and kept me worried until I left the office the night before the trip.

But now, as our trip was ending and our final view of the river faded into the distance through the small window of the plane, I knew that the memories we had created would last forever, long after my day-to-day concerns at work were forgotten, and that the choice to go was one of the best decisions of my life.

This realization illustrates one of the greatest lessons in creating an extraordinary life: you must choose to create the memories that enrich your life.

Are you filling your life with moments worth remembering?

Think about the next few weeks on your calendar. Are they punctuated by special plans for an afternoon spent exclusively with one of your children, a surprise dinner with a close friend, or a weekend away with your spouse? Or is your calendar consumed by all the responsibilities of your life, leaving the special moments to happen completely by chance?

You Must Make Time for the Moments That Matter

Whether you work in an office, or you are creating a home and nurturing a family, it's easy to organize your life predominantly around all you have to do, believing that you will have time for the other things you want in your life when your work is done. But have you ever reached that point? I haven't.

No matter how hard I work, or how organized, efficient, and productive I am, my work is never finished. Try sitting alone in your workspace and doing nothing for ten minutes. It's impossible. The phone will ring, e-mails will come in, and your coworkers will drop by asking, *Do you have a minute?* And just ask any mother anywhere on the planet if her work is ever done. You'll get a clear answer, I promise.

Unceasing demand is a reality of life and you're probably not going to change it. But what you can do—what you must do—is decide whether you're going to let that be the story of your life. It happens all the time and it happens to good, caring people.

People whose lives are dominated by work usually don't intend to live that way; they have families, causes, and interests outside of work that they really plan to get to *someday when work settles down.* But it never does. The story of their lives becomes one of taking their computers on vacation and getting lost in urgent e-mails while their family plays on the beach, or checking their BlackBerries constantly while spouses or friends are trying to talk with them. Their lives become one long saga of missed ball games, cancelled lunches, late nights at the office, and weekends filled with work instead of rest and play.

Unfortunately, this lifestyle is also reinforced by recognition from the people around us. In the office, there are promotions, raises, plaques, and reserved parking spaces that await the highest achievers. In the home, the parent who drives the neighborhood carpool, volunteers to be room mother, leads the Brownie troop, and organizes the silent auction, as well as all the endless cooking, cleaning, and managing that a family requires, can receive so much praise that he or she approaches martyrdom.

It's addictive and it's hard to give up all the acceptance and praise that come when you're giving everything to the responsibilities of your life. But is it really the life you want?

I'm not saying that these responsibilities are not important; of course they are. Your job, whatever it may be, is essential to your life, to your family, and to the people you care about. It's also one of the most important ways you utilize the talent and opportunity you've been given and, hopefully, it's a job you love.

But the question is: *Are you intentionally making time for the special moments you will want to remember?* Because if you aren't focused on making them happen, they won't, at least not with any regularity. And one day, you will regret it.

Change Your Perspective

Here's a simple exercise to drive home the importance of planning special times in the midst of your busy schedule: Can you remember your specific challenges at work for this same month last year? The things you were worried about, the deadlines you had to meet, and how important it all seemed? Probably not.

Now, think about what you do remember from last year.

Most likely, you only remember the moments that really mattered. They might be moments you shared with coworkers or with loved ones, big events or smaller, more intimate moments; some might be painful, while others are moments of real joy and connection with the people you love. But this is probably all that you remember from an entire year of your life. In essence, *these memorable moments were your life, the rest was just details.* And realizing this will forever change your perspective on the importance of creating them.

Why not create a life that is filled with memories of treasured moments?

What do you want your children to remember? The day you took off from work to spend exclusively with them, the night you took them to hear their favorite band in concert, or the adventure trip they will never forget?

What do you want the people on your team at work to remember? The special recognition you took time to give them at a company meeting or the afternoon you spent offering them personal mentoring?

These special memories, and all the others you want your life to include, won't happen unless you make time to create them. You can create a life that is rich with special moments and real connection with the people you care about, but to do it, you must take action.

Begin to Create the Moments You Will Treasure

Start by opening your calendar right now and making time in the coming week for an experience that will one day be a treasured memory. Make an appointment with yourself to bring flowers home to your spouse this week. If you've promised to attend a ball game or an event for one of your children, block your calendar open for an extra hour before the time you need to leave so that nothing unexpected can make you late. If you have a close friend with whom you haven't talked lately, schedule time on your calendar to call him or her, and mark it as an important conference call.

When my children were young, I had them maintain a list of fun things they would like for us to do. We referred to it as the *Oh Boy!* list, because every time we chose to do one of the activities they had listed, their immediate response was "Oh Boy!" My goal was to do one of the activities on that list each week and the memories we created are some of my most treasured.

When you begin to build these kinds of moments into your life, you will be surprised at how much value the people around you place on small things. You'll quickly learn that what matters are not the big vacations or the expensive gifts you can provide. In fact, too much value is placed on these things, especially when you really know you're doing them to compensate for all that you haven't done.

What the people in your life treasure is *you.* They value an hour of your undivided attention as much as a trip to the beach—a spontaneous stop for ice cream that includes seeing you relaxed and laughing, as much as buying them a present.

These are the real gifts you can give them, and in the process, you'll create the memories that enrich their life and yours.

At the end of our river trip, Scott, Sarah, and I purchased three identical silver amulets made by one of the river guides. They each contain a Native American symbol representing the Middle Fork of the Salmon River where we had spent the past six days. Since we returned, mine has never left my neck, and they've continuously worn theirs.

As I'm writing these words, I can touch that amulet and be instantly transported to a rich set of memories that are some of the most treasured of my life, and I know that they can too. I would not have these memories if I had not consciously chosen to create them, despite my dedication to my work and the demands on me.

And today, I would not trade those memories for all the money in the world. They sustain me and give me strength when I need it most.

CHARACTER VERSUS IMAGE

Who are you when no one is watching?

A gain!" my Taekwondo instructor shouted, commanding the class to another repetition of the fighting combination we were learning. The moves were difficult and I was already tired from a long day at work. With each repetition, my arms and legs felt heavier and I began to hold back, conserving my energy while hoping that no one noticed. Because I was the highest-ranking black belt, I had the senior position on the mat in front of two dozen students; a position where my every move was visible and expected to be an example for others to follow.

As my instructor moved among us, inspecting each person's form and technique, I was careful to give my best when he was near and then rest when he walked away. In this way, I believed I was maintaining my image as the senior student without actually having to exert the effort. It was in one of these moments of executing the movements half-heartedly that I was surprised by the whispered voice of my instructor close behind me.

"Who are you when no one is watching, Mr. Huling?"

Even now, I can recall how I felt at that moment. At the instant I heard his voice I realized that there was no shame in being tired or unable to perform at my highest level; the shame was in trying to uphold an image that wasn't true.

Have you ever tried this same approach? Can you remember a time when you had lost all passion for the work you were doing, but put on an image of energy and false enthusiasm for the people around you? Perhaps you can remember sustaining an image in a relationship, portraying a personal connection that you no longer felt or feigning dedication to a community service project that in truth had become a dreaded burden.

No matter when or where it happens, the moment you shift your energy toward maintaining your image—crafting your actions and your words to sustain the appearance of something that isn't true—you compromise your most valuable attribute: the content of your character.

If this is where you are, there are three important things to remember.

Remember that the people around you usually know the truth, in spite of your efforts to conceal it. They have built-in radar for inconsistencies and subtle cues that tell them the smile on your face isn't matched by the feeling in your heart.

While you may not yet be ready to resign from the job or end the relationship, you can stop exhausting yourself to convince them that everything's great. Instead, begin to be more authentic in what you say and do. Don't say yes when you mean no, compliment only what you truly respect, and pause to consider whether each action you are about to take aligns with your personal values for honesty and integrity.

Remember that if perfection were the requirement, no one would succeed. People around you face their own fear of inadequacy and rejection, and like you, are tempted to create a better version of themselves through the image they want you to see.

But if you will begin to acknowledge your own imperfections—that you don't always make the right choice and aren't always in control of every situation—you will not only drop your own image and become more authentic, you'll set others free to accept their imperfections as well.

Remember that the image you are sustaining is actually a reflection of the person you want to become. When you create an image of passionate engagement with your work, it's because you really want your work, and your life, to have these qualities. Instead of pretending that you love your job, channel that same energy into a written vision of what you really want and then commit to finding an opportunity that takes you toward it.

Let this simple Latin phrase become the standard for your life: "Esse quam videre," meaning "To be, rather than to appear." When you do, you will discover that the person you truly are is actually greater than the image you tried to create.

THE HIGH PRICE OF PERFECTION

Live by realistic standards to renew your energy and enthusiasm

I glimpsed the black leather boxing glove an instant before it landed solidly on my right temple. Although less than full strength, the blow made my knees buckle and sent a shower of sparks across my brain.

I was training with the world champion kickboxer, Philip Botha, who was instructing me on a technique that I couldn't seem to master. My irritation grew with each failed attempt until finally I did what no fighter should ever do: I dropped my hands in complete frustration. And that was when he hit me. Like all great teachers, his intention was to drive home an important lesson.

"Do you see what you're doing?" he asked as I tried to clear my head. "You're expecting to be perfect and when you're not, you give up in frustration. When you do that, you learn nothing and you miss all the fun."

It was a message I would not forget, because it taught me one of the greatest lessons in choosing my life: the high price of perfection.

Do you expect to be perfect?

Many of you would say no, but your real answer can be seen in how you respond when you fall short of your expectations. For example, when someone compliments you on a personal achievement, do you deflect the compliment by focusing on the one thing that wasn't perfect? Do you mentally replay your mistakes, going over and over them as if you could somehow go back and avoid them? Do you set goals that are unrealistic and then berate yourself when you fall short?

These are examples of the high price of perfection, of measuring yourself against a standard you can never meet. Every time you do this, you pay a price in terms of lost energy, diminished confidence, and a reduced quality of life. And in the words of my teacher, you learn nothing and you're missing all the fun.

Set a Realistic Standard

You can avoid many of the problems of perfection by beginning with a realistic standard. Before you set a goal, ask yourself what an objective definition of success would be. Take into consideration all the factors that will influence your ability to reach it, such as how much experience you have, the new skills you will have to learn, and the resources you have available. Then, set a goal that represents your best possible performance given these factors. Goals that are both challenging and realistic inspire you to stretch and grow. Expecting perfection only sets you up for disappointment and defeat.

Learn to Keep Score

Developing a method of tracking your progress is one of the most important tools in avoiding perfectionism. You know that reaching any goal consists of repeatedly taking several steps forward and at least one back. But unless you keep score, you'll be tempted to view every step back as a failure instead of seeing it in the context of all you've achieved so far. Keeping score also enables you to celebrate your success at different points along the way, instead of waiting until the goal is reached.

Plan to Stay Engaged

If you were perfect, you would pursue your goal with dedication and enthusiasm every day. But the reality is that at some point you will be tired, or your inspiration will simply lag. When this happens, as it does to all of us, you will need to reach for resources that can help you. But they will be available only if you plan ahead.

For example, I have a folder in my desk of special letters, cards and e-mails that I have received over the years about my leadership and my impact on the people around me. When I encounter a moment of self-doubt, I can always take out that folder and begin reading. In only a few minutes, my spirits lift and I'm ready to get back in the game. Take time to plan for the resources you will need before you actually need them. If I had waited until I was down, it would have been too late to begin collecting the items in my folder.

Start today to move from suffering the defeat of perfectionism to enjoying the energy and confidence of meeting the goals you set.

THE CURE FOR EXHAUSTION

Build deeper connections to ignite meaning, purpose, and pride in your work

W*arning! Your connection has been lost. You must reestablish your connection to continue working.*

It was almost midnight when the message flashed across my computer screen. I was alone in my office, working on a report that was due the next day. I was tired and had no time to waste. But now, I was forced to stop, staring at the message that had unexpectedly interrupted my typing.

Your connection has been lost. There was truth in those words that went far beyond my company's computer network. For months I had been conscious of a growing emptiness as I worked each day.

On the surface nothing had changed. I had a position that many would envy and I was working for a good company that valued my contribution. But where once my job had been an exciting adventure, it had somehow become an obligation that now I had to force myself to fulfill.

Although I could still remember a time when I was excited to begin each day—a time when I faced both the challenges and the successes of my work with enthusiasm—I was now caught in a spiral that was slowly taking me down.

Are you in this same spiral? Do you feel more exhausted each day from the effort to fulfill this dimension of your life? Whether you're leading a team at work, teaching a classroom of students, or managing a household, it will happen to each of us. And when it does, there is only one answer, an answer that is one of the greatest lessons in choosing your life.

You must reestablish your connection. Without the energy and inspiration of a real connection to your work, you will never experience the success, or the fulfillment, you want. But once you find it, it can fuel a level of performance beyond your imagination.

Find a Deeper Connection to The People around You

Do you really know the people with whom you work closely? Do you feel that you are part of a team, or are you an outsider with little sense of belonging?

You can start today to build a connection to the people you work with by simply listening. Listen to their thoughts and ideas, as well as the stories about their families and their lives. When you're in a meeting, really listen to what they have to say without processing other background thoughts, interrupting, or checking your BlackBerry.

The more you do this, the more you will create a connection of understanding and trust between you, a connection that will give you a sense of belonging and inclusion that can become one of the most important elements of the work you do.

Find a Deeper Connection to Your Personal Excellence

Are you proud of the work you do? If not, challenge yourself to reach a higher standard. When you choose a personal standard, such as "I will keep every commitment I make," you set in motion a force that establishes what's important to you and makes you accountable for living up to it. The pride you feel when you set a standard for excellence, and then achieve it, will forge a powerful personal connection to your work.

Find a Deeper Connection to Your Real Purpose

Do you see your work as part of something important? If I view my job of running a staffing company as simply a series of business goals and financial objectives, I tap into only a fraction of the passion I feel when I remember instead that our real purpose is finding jobs for people who need them. Seeing a larger purpose in what you do brings inspiration to even the most mundane tasks and connects you to your work in a deeply meaningful way.

Sitting in my office that night I vowed to reestablish my connection to the work I was doing and, in the end, I was successful. But in the process, I learned something vitally important.

The real cure for exhaustion is not rest. The cure for exhaustion is establishing a wholehearted connection to what you do. This connection will give you the sustaining energy of meaning, purpose, and pride not only in your work, but in who you are.

HAS YOUR JOB BECOME BIGGER
THAN YOUR LIFE?

Take a personal and professional inventory to restore your balance

The headline in the morning newspaper instantly drew my attention to the article below. Less than twenty-four hours ago a prominent local attorney had taken his life. Bob was a man I had known casually through various professional associations and a few deals between our companies. He was very competent; I remembered how detailed he was in the negotiations we had conducted. As I read on, I learned that he had a wife and two children, now left behind in the horrific wake of his actions the day before.

Over the next few weeks, Bob's suicide was the topic of much discussion, and through various friends and contacts, I learned the story of what happened. Bob had been working on a very large deal, one that would merge his company with a competitor, creating a dominant player in the market. For almost a year, the merger had been his sole focus and he had worked as much as one hundred hours each week, even resorting to sleeping some nights in his office.

At the final hour, the other company decided to abort the merger. No one knew that when Bob left the office that day he would never return. Distraught, disillusioned, hopeless—all of these emotions must have overwhelmed him, and in the end, he took his own life.

Bob's story had a profound impact on me. Somehow, he had allowed the circumstances of his job to become so important, that when they failed, he felt his life was over. It was a mistake I was determined to avoid, in my own life, and in the lives of everyone I could influence.

Are Your Responsibilities Overwhelming You?

Everyone is being asked to do more today than they were a few years ago and often with fewer resources. While you need to stretch and grow to be successful, there is also a point where the impossibility of your workload can overwhelm you.

Instead of becoming immobilized, take control by making an inventory of everything you're working on, and then take note of the deadlines, the level of effort required, and the resources you will need to be successful. Use this inventory to realistically assess what you can do and then start to let others know where you need help. The risk you may feel in stating that you can't do it all is far less than the risk you're taking, personally and professionally, by trying and then failing.

Are You Secretly Afraid You're Not Qualified?

People with significant responsibilities have at least once had the fear that they aren't smart or talented enough to meet the demands of their job. As soon as you have this feeling, your next fear is that someone will find out. It's a natural reaction and one that, if left to grow, will undermine your energy and your confidence. The antidote to this fear is disclosure.

When I first became a CEO, I reviewed financial reports that I didn't always understand. Although I needed to understand the reports, I was embarrassed to admit that I didn't, for fear that I wouldn't seem qualified. As soon as I asked for help, others were happy to give it, and a fear that might have disabled me was relieved.

Is There No Room in Your Schedule for Your Life?

Take a look at the week that's ahead and pretend it's the calendar of a stranger. What can you conclude about the life it reveals? Is there time designated for a family event such as a ball game or a movie? Are there entries for dinner or buying a special gift for a spouse or partner? What about time for exercise, prayer or lunch with a friend? The absence of items like these is an early warning sign of exhaustion and burnout.

Although several years have now passed, I still wonder what might have happened if Bob had asked and answered questions like these. Unfortunately, I will never know.

But if he could speak to us now, I believe he would say something like this: *Dedicate yourself wholeheartedly to your work, but never allow your job to become bigger than your life.* I hope we're all listening.

ARE YOU CREATING YOUR OWN CRISIS?

Control your pace to raise the quality of your work

I was already late when I left the office heading for the airport. My flight was the last one that day that would enable me to have dinner with an important client in a distant city, and I had to make it.

Driving well above the speed limit, I could feel my hands tighten around the steering wheel. My pulse was throbbing in my temples as the stress of missing my flight began to rise. When another driver attempted to cross over into my lane I accelerated to close the gap between my car and the one in front of me, blocking him.

Speeding around a curve in the highway I suddenly saw a sea of red brake lights ahead, forcing me to a complete stop. Soon, I heard sirens and saw the flashing lights of two ambulances racing down the shoulder of the highway.

When I finally reached the accident, it was a vision of total devastation. One car was overturned and several others lay crumpled at odd angles while emergency personnel hurried from one injured person to another.

Staring in shock at this terrible tragedy, I witnessed a scene I had watched many times on television, but never in reality. Barely twenty feet in front of me, two emergency workers lifted the body of a man and placed him into a long, white bag. They pulled the zipper from foot to head with a slowness that seemed almost reverent, closing the body within it and closing the journey of a life.

Even as the shrill command of a policeman's whistle forced me to drive on, I knew that image would stay with me forever.

Had the man in that bag been in a hurry, just as I was? Was he driving too fast, dialing his cell phone, or mentally distracted by a problem at work when his last moment occurred? I'll never know. But I will always suspect that it was the same frenzied pace that I felt—the same urgent need to hurry that created the devastation on that highway.

Except for a few minutes difference in time, and the miracle of grace, the man in that bag could have been me.

Are you always hurrying through your life? Is your pace so urgent that you become angry at the smallest delay like a lengthy traffic light or a customer in front of you counting out exact change to pay? If so, then here are two questions you should consider.

Are You Creating Your Own Crisis?

On that day, making my flight was so urgent that I felt compelled to drive dangerously, but it was a crisis I had made myself by squeezing in one additional meeting before I left. Today, I can't even remember what that meeting was about, but the urgency it created could have cost me my life.

Instead, why not plan adequate time for the things you need to do and leave a small buffer between commitments for the unexpected? As radical as this may sound, you will actually get more done by remaining in a calmer, focused state than you will by rushing frantically from commitment to commitment.

Are You Always Distracted?

Constant multitasking only creates the illusion of productivity, not the results, while adding extra stress. I recently received a call from a colleague about a complex financial spreadsheet. In the background, I could hear the sounds of a crowd cheering. When I asked, he told me he was at his daughter's soccer game and how important it was to her that he was there to watch her play.

I realized this man was sitting in the stands with his laptop open, discussing an issue on his cell phone, while believing he was fulfilling an important commitment to his child. The sad truth was that both his work, and his daughter, received less than his best that day.

The commitments you make and the people to whom you make them are essential elements in creating the life you want to live. Slow down enough to give them the time and the undivided focus they deserve, and you will find that both your work and your relationships reach a new level of success and fulfillment.

EMBRACING INTERRUPTIONS

An open door to enhance your life

I heard a brief knock on my office door before Susan stepped in asking, "Have you got a minute?" Looking up into the troubled face of a person who was both an employee and a friend, I had an inner reaction that was all too familiar: "Oh great, what's wrong now?"

It was a reaction that Susan would never have detected, because I smiled and said, "Sure, what can I do to help?" And then I spent the next forty-five minutes listening and offering suggestions on a problem she was facing. When we finished, we had not only developed a good plan for addressing her issue, we had also strengthened our relationship. It was a productive meeting with a great result.

But when she left my office, I started to think about my initial reaction; a reaction that I could remember having not only at work, but at home and with friends, as well.

Have you ever had the same reaction? I suspect, like all of us, you have. In the workplace, requests for "a minute" are so commonplace that you can seldom get through a day without one. Similar requests can come from your spouse, your friends, or one of your children. And with uncanny accuracy, they arrive when it's least convenient, whether you're engrossed in your own responsibilities or you've just settled down for a few quiet moments of rest.

Regardless of the source or the timing, interruptions can be frustrating. And yet, like my experience with Susan, interruptions that have frustrated me initially have often led to some of my most satisfying and fulfilling moments. Understanding this paradox taught me one of the greatest lessons I've learned in over half a century of living: the importance of embracing interruptions.

Before you dismiss this advice as applying only to those with plenty of free time and flexibility, let me remind you that my life is as hectic and full as yours. Each week I balance my *LifeDimensions* as husband, dad,

JIM HULING

CEO, martial artist, author, speaker, and friend. I carefully plan each week in advance and fill my calendar the way you would pack a suitcase for a long trip, with every space designated for some purpose.

And yet, learning to embrace interruptions, to welcome them as openings to the most meaningful moments, has enhanced my life beyond measure. The next time you feel frustrated by an interruption, here are a few things to remember.

Life Doesn't Conform to Your Schedule

The people in your life need you when the crisis occurs, not when you can fit them in. When a friend receives a frightening diagnosis, or a member of your team detects a project about to go off track, you can't say, "I've got an opening next Tuesday, can we talk then?" You find a way to be there for them in the same way you would expect them to be there for you. And when the situation is reversed, they will be likely to reciprocate.

People Come to You Because They Believe You Can Help and That You Care

The day they stop coming, you've either lost your value or you've convinced them that they don't matter to you. Remember that leading is more about actions than words. Whether it's your children or your teammates, stopping to help them solve a problem clearly communicates that they are important to you. And when you look back on your leadership and your life, the moments you stopped to help will be the ones you cherish most.

Staying Accessible and Available Keeps You Engaged

Isolation and burnout are two of the most common factors that can lead you to disengage mentally, physically, and even spiritually. Interruptions force you to reengage with the people in your life, to get outside the narrow circle of your own thoughts and schedule, and to find the renewed energy that sharing a challenge, as well as a triumph with people you care about, will bring.

While you will always need times of focused concentration, learn to embrace interruptions when they occur. The knock on your door could be the beginning of your next great experience in choosing your life.

CHOOSE CAREFULLY WHAT YOU CARRY

Are You Compromising Your Life's Journey?

Backpackers are an unusual breed of campers. They venture into the wilderness carrying on their backs everything they need for survival. Food, shelter, clothing, and even water are stuffed into their brightly colored packs and hauled for miles before the perfect campsite is found.

If my pack had contained only those essential things on my first trip, I would have missed one of the great lessons in choosing my life. But I had also crammed into my pack extra food, extra clothes, a pillow, a comfortable camp chair, books, soft slippers, and a bottle of good wine to enhance my camping experience. By the second mile, I was disgorging my pack of everything that wasn't absolutely necessary just to survive.

Fortunately, lessons in backpacking are learned quickly. For my second trip I spent more time evaluating the weight versus the worth of each item I packed. I ended up with fewer comforts and more pleasure on each step of the trail. As my experience grew, I learned to sense the real value of each item in terms of the cost of carrying it.

Today, I will always bring the things that mean the most to me, including some indulgences, but I have consistently pared away the things that I do not really need, the things that weigh me down without being truly important.

In choosing your life, you can often find yourself exhausted from the weight of the things you carry. Did you feel it this morning as you faced another day? Was your first thought about how tired you were and all that you had to do before you could rest? Perhaps it's time to take a look in your pack at all that you are carrying.

Anger and Resentment

If you're carrying them, you're paying a high price. Even if you were truly wronged or harmed by someone, carrying the weight of your bitterness will exhaust you.

You withhold your forgiveness as a means of revenge, but usually the person who harmed you is unaffected by it. Meanwhile you carry the weight of it through every step you take. Forgiveness is a gift you give yourself and it has the miraculous effect of emptying your pack of a heavy burden that can finally be left on the ground behind you.

Indulgent Comforts
Like the bottle of wine on my first trip, indulgent comforts can also be heavy items. You enjoy them, but when do you stop to consider whether they are worth the cost?

You work longer and harder to surround yourself with a bigger house, a newer car, personal trainers, and exotic vacations without ever measuring their return in real happiness. Each of these things can bring pleasure, but cumulatively they add a weight that you must carry. Like a backpacker, you must choose them carefully.

Abandoned Dreams
These can be the heaviest burden of all. When you load your pack with every expectation of your parents, your bosses, and your culture about what you should do, where you should live, how you should think and feel, you leave no room for the things that are truly yours, the things that make the journey your own.

Did you have a dream once? Was there something you wanted to do before all the responsibilities and demands of your life took you down a different path? If you can remember it, then it is still within you, and you are carrying it every day. Taking the smallest action to revive your dreams will transform them from a weight to a source of joy and energy.

Be Wary of Dead Weight
Everything you choose to carry through your life has a price. Building meaningful relationships, engaging in work that honors your talent, and living with integrity are things that bring a return in health and happiness many times greater than the investment you make. But others simply add weight. "Dead weight" describes them perfectly. The more of them you carry, the closer you are to being dead, physically, emotionally, and spiritually.

Stop today to take a look at the contents of your pack. You just might find a lot of things that you no longer choose to carry.

INVEST YOUR ENERGY IN
WHAT MATTERS MOST

*Do you manage your most vital resource as well as you plan your
time?*

You're not really listening to me, are you?" The question snapped my attention back to the executive who was briefing me on an issue. Although I was tempted to deny it, I knew it was true. I wasn't really listening and I couldn't even remember when I had stopped.

We were at the end of a long day filled with non-stop meetings, including a team meeting over sandwiches at lunch. Technically, I had time for this final meeting—the slot was open on my calendar—but what I didn't have was energy.

"No, I'm not," I confessed to my teammate who, fortunately for me, was also my friend. "I'm exhausted and I just don't have the energy left to give you or this issue the attention you deserve. I'm sorry."

In that moment, I realized I had scheduled the meeting without considering the implied commitment I was making to focus and engage at a high level at the end of a very long day. As a result, I made a promise to a person who mattered, on an issue that mattered, that I could not fulfill.

The disappointment on the face of my teammate taught me one of the greatest lessons in choosing your life: the importance of managing your energy.

Has this ever happened to you? Have you ever found yourself with available time, but without the energy, focus or passion that you needed? Whether in a business meeting, or engaging with a spouse or child at the end of your day, it has happened to all of us. And when it does, you often disappoint the people who matter most.

Map Your Energy as You Map Your Time

Compare this way of managing your energy with the way you manage your time. Would you commit to a two-hour meeting if you had only thirty minutes available? Of course not. But you routinely make commitments for energy that are equally unrealistic because you don't evaluate them as closely.

If you want to be truly successful, you must learn to pace your energy with the same careful planning that you do your time.

Take a look at the next particularly busy day on your calendar and place a number between one and five beside each meeting or activity to indicate the energy that will be required, where five represents the highest level.

Now, evaluate the pacing of your day. Is it realistic?

Many times you schedule consecutive meetings where the energy requirement is level five and believe that you can sustain that level of concentration and engagement throughout all of them without any need for recovery. This is usually self-deception. Even though you may want to perform at your peak all day, the people around you can see that your energy is progressively declining.

Mapping your energy requirements, and then realistically evaluating your capacity, will help ensure that the promises you make are ones you can keep.

Pay Attention to the Energy You Need at Home

And what about your commitment to those outside of work? If you were asked whether your work was more important than your family, most of you would quickly say no. But paradoxically, you deplete yourself throughout the day on the unconscious assumption that your family and friends don't need your prime energy.

Choose one day this week to imagine you have an important meeting with your boss scheduled that evening and then watch how you automatically reserve enough energy to be at your best. Do the people you care about most deserve anything less? You'll be surprised at how much it means to them when you ensure you have energy left at the end of the day to give.

Expand Your Energy Capacity

Finally, remember also that your energy capacity can be expanded to be greater than it is today. Focusing on the people and activities that strengthen you and enrich your life, such as exercise, prayer, time alone and close interaction with those you love, will not only replenish you, they will increase your ability to create the life you want.

Begin today to take personal responsibility for how you invest your energy and you'll be amazed at the results.

REACH YOUR INTENDED DESTINATION

Set precise goals and then act on the guidance you receive

Y*ou have arrived at your destination,"* the semi-robotic voice droned from my car's navigational system. If I hadn't been driving for the past hour, I would have laughed.

Instead of arriving at the office building where I was to meet an important client, I was instead staring at the loading dock of a deserted warehouse. I had faithfully followed each instruction issued by the system, from taking major highways to making individual turns down isolated streets, but in the process had become totally lost. Not only was I about to miss an important meeting, but in perfect irony, my only way out was to use the same navigational system that had brought me there.

Although this was not the first unhappy experience in my love-hate relationship with a navigational system, it illustrates one of the greatest lessons in choosing your life.

Have you ever found yourself in a life situation that was different than you intended?

Did you begin with a vision for your career that has now gone off course, leaving you stranded in a job where you have no real passion or opportunity? Did you give your best effort to a project or assignment, doing all the right things, only to see it fail in the end?

If you have, then you know the pain and frustration that come when your life navigation system fails. To get back on course, you must ask, and answer, two important questions.

Do You Know Your Exact Destination?

As I sat in the warehouse parking lot, I realized that I had entered the correct street name into my car's navigation system, *Havenwood*, but had failed to include the word "lane." Without that additional detail, the system led me to the same address on Havenwood *Court,* a destination far from where I wanted to go.

Just as this small detail navigated me to the wrong location, the lack of precision in your goals can easily take you off track. For example, have you ever accepted a position where you received the title and the compensation you wanted, only to later realize that other factors such as the integrity of the company or the level of decision-making latitude given made it the wrong place for you? The disappointment you experienced could have been avoided if you had been clear about all the factors that were crucial in your decision to take the job.

Take time to really think about the goal you're pursuing so that your focus is clear and precise. Develop written answers to questions such as: *Why is this goal important to me? What is it I really want to achieve? How will I know when I've succeeded?*

When you become clear about your exact destination, you increase the likelihood that you will actually arrive.

Are You Following Your Guidance System?

When I've entered the correct destination, my car's navigational system will then warn me if I'm off track, issuing commands such as: *"You have left the route. Please turn around."*

Your life navigation system works in the same way. In whatever goal you're pursuing, you are receiving guidance all the time. A mentor may offer you advice on a challenging problem you're facing; a friend can compassionately share a painful truth that you need to hear; or more importantly, your heart will tell you if what you're doing is not who you really are.

Your challenge is not in being guided. Guidance is all around you. Your challenge is in listening, and acting on, the guidance you receive.

Start by capturing the advice and insight you receive in a notebook or on your computer, adding your own thoughts about what it means to you and what you plan to do with it. The simple act of writing it down dramatically increases your ability to remember and utilize the information, and in the process, will guide you to stay on course.

When you take the step of adding clarity to the goals you're pursuing, and start to really heed the guidance you receive, you will begin to create the life you want.

PART IV—MY WISH FOR YOU

A final story on creating an extraordinary life

*S*eptember 17, 1937. A date that probably holds no significance for you, but one that made all the difference in my life. On that date, a young man named Bill, recently discharged from the Army, married a girl named Ann. They were like any other married couple, then or now, with great dreams for their life together and the youthful optimism to believe that everything they dreamed of would come true.

Their first enterprise was to open a little shop that sold caramel corn. While Bill worked on the machine that popped and mixed the corn, Ann perfected the caramel recipe, and together they created a small, but thriving business. This venture led to other career paths and interests, but along the way they began to realize that they had a larger dream, one that became the single focus of their lives. That dream was to have a child.

One year passed, and then another and another, and still their dream was not realized. Without the aid of modern science to diagnose or assist the process, they were forced to simply keep trying and remain hopeful. In all, seventeen years would go by as they waited, and hoped, and prayed for the gift of a child. And then one day, a miracle happened. The child for whom they had waited so long was born and that child was me.

The next five years were filled with all the joy and love that Bill and Ann had imagined as they wove their lives around their roles as parents. Then one day, Ann began to have unusual symptoms and sought the advice of our family doctor. Tests were run and the diagnosis was confirmed. Ann had terminal, inoperable cancer.

Because the cancer had already spread to her lymph nodes, she was given only weeks to live. After waiting seventeen years to have her child, she now faced the certain knowledge that the past five years were all she would ever know as a mother.

As she later told me the story, she sat alone in her hospital bed one night almost to the point of despair, and began to pray a single prayer.

Her prayer was that she be allowed to see me grow to become a man. In her life, she would ask for nothing else but this, she bargained with God. I can only imagine the ferocity of that prayer and the sincerity with which it was offered from a mother's heart.

Within days, her cancer went into remission. I'm sure there are others who would credit this to the wonderful doctors and the massive medications that were administered. Although she was grateful for them, my mother saw them as only the instruments of an answered prayer. A prayer that had brought her what she wanted most in the world.

The next seventeen years were as wonderful, and as ordinary, as they are in the life of every family. And although they saw the passing of my father, they also included all the moments of school plays and family vacations, measles and chicken pox, bicycle accidents, first dates, and missed curfews that the raising of children brings. It was a full, rich life that in reflection condenses down to a handful of cherished memories.

One of these memories is of a Sunday morning as I was excitedly preparing for my college graduation, my mind filled with a rosy vision of my future, and all that my life would include as I went out into the world.

Over the preceding weeks, I had casually noticed that my mother was often tired and seemed to not be herself. Today, she could not walk. Within a few hours, she was hospitalized. The cancer had returned and she was given only a few weeks to live. She was placed in a special hospital room that included a sofa so that I could be with her around the clock. My senior classes were placed on hold as I spent day and night with her absorbing all that I could of the time we had left.

One morning, very near the end, I sat on the side of her bed overcome with my emotions. I could not believe that her life could be ending just as mine was really beginning. There was so much that I wanted to do and to become, and I wanted her to share in every moment of it. I poured out all that I felt and what I saw as the bitter unfairness of it all.

"It's not fair, it's just not fair," I said over and over again. To this day, I can feel my mother's hand on my head and hear her comforting voice.

"It is fair, son," she said. "In fact, it's more than fair."

I couldn't believe what I was hearing. How could she think it was fair that she would die at the very moment I was ready to launch my life? And this is when she told me the story of that night seventeen years ago and of her single prayer to see me grown.

"So you see, Jimmy," she said, "that's why I'm so happy. I got what I wanted."

Within days, she was gone. But this lesson became the defining message of my life, one that has stayed with me, shaping me, and guiding my path. And it is this lesson that evolved into the message of this book.

Who are you?
What do you really want?
What are you prepared to do?

These are the questions that can guide every aspect of your life, from your family and friends to the focus of your career. Through the pages of this book, you've learned all you need to know to create an extraordinary life. The rest is up to you.

My passionate, most cherished hope is that you will take what you've learned and apply it, work with it, change it to fit your vision, and ultimately, make it the life you actually live, not just the one you dream about.

You can create an extraordinary life. And when you do, you will one day know the joy and peace of being able to say in your final moments, *I got what I wanted.*

I know you will.

APPENDIX 1
Forms

The forms referred to throughout the text of the book are on the following pages:

1. *Who Am I?*
2. *What I Really Want*
3. *What I Am Prepared to Do*
4. *A Dream I Want to Awaken*
5. *Make Fear Your Ally*

A larger color version of each form is available for download at <u>www. JimHuling.com/forms</u>

JIMHULING.COM

Who Am I?

U *se the form to list the LifeDimensions you care most about. Remember to include everything, from family, to work, to personal activities as well as your involvement in causes that matter to you.*

The *LifeDimensions* That Are Important To Me:	5 Hours	Importance	Performance
1.			
2.			
3.			
4.			
5.			
6.			
7.			
8.			
9.			
10.			

Excerpts taken from

Choose your Life!

JIM HULING

What I Really Want

LifeDimension: _____

This form is designed to get your thoughts flowing and to open your heart to all you can imagine your life including. It won't be the final version of your LifeVision for this dimension, but it will help you discover some of your deepest desires so that you can include them when you write your complete vision.

In This Dimension Of My Life I Want To Be:

The first section focuses on what you want to be. When you work on this section, think of all the characteristics you want to embody in this dimension of your life and list them in the space provided.

_____

_____

_____

In This Dimension Of My Life These Are The Things I Want To Do:

Completing this section can be a lot of fun as you let your imagination picture all the things you'd like to do in this dimension of your life.

_____

_____

_____

In This Dimension Of My Life These Are The Things I Want To Learn:

Here's where you can envision the great lessons of your life and how you might apply them in this dimension. Think of the areas where knowledge, expertise, or wisdom will enable you to live the life you've imagined.

_____

_____

_____

Excerpts taken from

What I am Prepared To Do

It's time to start building your plan for the role you have chosen.

My Goal:
"First, you need to define your goal. Choose a goal that is both realistic and meaningful; a goal that represents a balance between the magnitude of what you want to accomplish and what you are certain you will actually do. Write it down in the space below."

_____

_____

I Will Keep Score By:
"For whatever goal you've chosen, you now need to create a method of tracking your results. Keeping score enables you to step up your efforts when you're falling behind, and celebrate when you're ahead. When you reach your goal, you will most likely feel that keeping score was your most valuable tool. Write down the ways in which you will keep score in pursuing this goal."

1. _____

2. _____

I Will Hold Myself Accountable By:
"Accountability is a powerful force, one that can give you the extra drive you may need during difficult times on the journey to fulfilling your vision. Write down exactly how you will hold yourself accountable on this particular goal."

1. _____

2. _____

I Will Stay Engaged By:
"Inevitably, you will reach a point in the journey toward your goal where you will be tired, under pressure in other areas, or where your inspiration for all you wanted to do simply lags. The moment when you are facing a crisis or a deep loss of motivation is the worst possible moment to think creatively about resources that could help. It is far better to plan now for those resources that can help you."

1. _____

2. _____

3. _____

Excerpts taken from

CHOOSE YOUR LIFE!

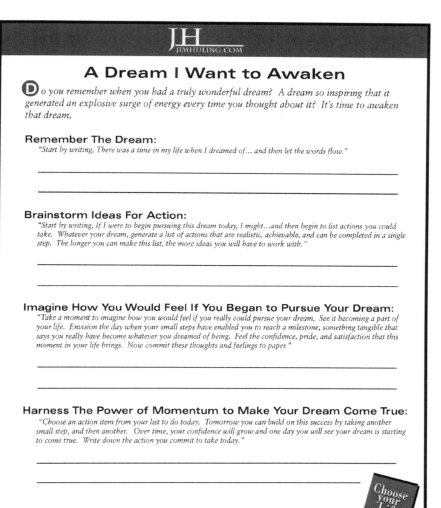

JH
JIMHULING.COM

A Dream I Want to Awaken

Do you remember when you had a truly wonderful dream? A dream so inspiring that it generated an explosive surge of energy every time you thought about it? It's time to awaken that dream.

Remember The Dream:
"Start by writing, There was a time in my life when I dreamed of... and then let the words flow."

Brainstorm Ideas For Action:
"Start by writing, If I were to begin pursuing this dream today, I might...and then begin to list actions you could take. Whatever your dream, generate a list of actions that are realistic, achievable, and can be completed in a single step. The longer you can make this list, the more ideas you will have to work with."

Imagine How You Would Feel If You Began to Pursue Your Dream:
"Take a moment to imagine how you would feel if you really could pursue your dream. See it becoming a part of your life. Envision the day when your small steps have enabled you to reach a milestone, something tangible that says you really have become whatever you dreamed of being. Feel the confidence, pride, and satisfaction that this moment in your life brings. Now commit these thoughts and feelings to paper."

Harness The Power of Momentum to Make Your Dream Come True:
"Choose an action item from your list to do today. Tomorrow you can build on this success by taking another small step, and then another. Over time, your confidence will grow and one day you will see your dream is starting to come true. Write down the action you commit to take today."

Excerpts taken from

Choose your Life!
JIM HULING

www.JimHuling.com

121

Make Fear Your Ally

If you use this process to make your fear an ally, you will find each fear to be either a warning enabling you to avoid real danger, or simply the small voice inside all of us that resists the unknown, a voice that you must acknowledge and move beyond if you are to grow and attempt great things.

State The Situation:
"Begin to clarify your fear by writing one or two sentences that describe the exact situation."

_____

_____

Bring Out Your Fears:
"Begin to list everything bad that could happen. Don't be an optimist; get it all out on paper in the most vivid, excruciating detail you can imagine. Assess how likely each one is to actually happen. To do this, place a letter beside each fear (R-realistic, U-unrealistic, N-never)."

_____

_____

Envision The Outcome You Want Most:
"Begin to envision all that you want to happen, all that will and can happen, when you face this challenge and succeed. See yourself looking back one day at all the fears that might have kept you imprisoned. Feel the self-respect, confidence, and sense of personal power you now have because you chose to overcome them. Write down everything you think and feel in this moment."

_____

_____

Make A Choice:
"You need to listen to your fears, but you must also weigh them against the passion and hope of your outcome. Ultimately, you must decide whether your fear is helping you or holding you back. Now, write down what you have decided to do, and why."

_____

_____

Excerpts taken from

Choose your Life!

JIM HULING

www.JimHuling.com